- What is abnormal sex?
- Do particular foods or drugs pep up the sex drive?
- How long can sperm live?
- Do boys have a different interest in sex from girls?
- What does the expression "female trouble" mean?

With this book you won't have to be afraid of the questions—or the answers.

WARDELL B. POMEROY received the A.B. and M.A. in psychology from Indiana University and the Ph.D. from Columbia University. As research associate at the Institute for Sex Research, he was co-author with the late Alfred Kinsey of *Sexual Behavior in the Human Male* and *Sexual Behavior in the Human Female*. He is academic dean at the Institute for Advanced Study of Human Sexuality in San Francisco, California, where he lives with his family.

GIRLS
AND
SEX

Wardell B. Pomeroy, Ph.D.
Co-author of the Kinsey Reports

Published by
Dell Publishing Co., Inc.
1 Dag Hammarskjold Plaza
New York, New York 10017

Laurl-Leaf Library ® TM 766734,
Dell Publishing Co., Inc.

ISBN: 0-440-92904-0

RL: 9.8
Printed in the United States of America
First Laurel-Leaf printing—December 1981
Second Laurel-Leaf printing—January 1982

A hardcover edition of this work is available through
Delacorte Press, 1 Dag Hammarskjold Plaza,
New York, New York.

Contents

Preface to the
Second Edition

In the eleven years since this book was first published (I write now in 1980) there has been a great social change in the area of human sexuality. It isn't the so-called "sexual revolution" we've heard so much about. That phrase is a misnomer when it's used to imply that people are having a great deal more free and uninhibited sex. The fact is that the *rate* of increase has not altered in any significant way, adjusting to social evolution and the growth of population as it always has. Nor are people indulging in more *kinds* of sexual activity; what human beings (and animals) do sexually has always been done. But what *has* changed is the acceptance by the general population of sexual activity and sexual language that was unacceptable in the Fifties and the beginning of the Sixties. We see this freedom in books, magazines, and motion pictures—even to some extent in television.

While both sexes have been affected by this profound change, girls have felt it far more than boys. The women's movement has been largely responsible for revising public attitudes toward the role of women in social and economic life—even including indiscriminate use of the word "girls." (I use it here because it is surely applicable to the early teenagers and preteenagers for whom this book is written.) Obviously, so great a change must be reflected in this revision of my book, but it has generated confusion and difficulties as well, and it is my hope that I will be able to put the whole matter into perspective in the pages that follow.

I have drawn not only upon the resources and professional colleagues cited in the first edition, but on those acquired in the intervening decade. To all of these individuals, I extend my renewed gratitude and thanks. As in *Boys and Sex*, I have had the collaboration of John Tebbel, who has done the actual writing and helped to clarify my thoughts.

I want also to offer renewed thanks to my wife, Martha, to whom this book is dedicated. We read and reread the original manuscript to each other, which proved most helpful in correcting errors of omission, commission, and emphasis, and she again has been a constant source of support in the preparation of this revision.

Wardell Pomeroy

Introduction

If you're a teenage girl today, it's quite possible you may be troubled and confused, at least to a certain extent, about sex. If it's any consolation, the probability is that your parents may share your feelings. As you are, they're aware of the new climate of sexual freedom and acceptance, and they don't know how much to tell you about sex, or even whether to tell you anything at all, relying on school, church, friends, or a combination of all these to provide the necessary information.

Your generation has grown up a lot faster than previous ones. When I first wrote this book, more than a decade ago, not many girls younger than thirteen or fourteen would have read it. Now, girls of ten, eleven, and twelve could be expected to read and understand it. Girls today read about sex in books written for them, especially those by authors like Judy Blume, and they can easily find access to information about it in adult books, magazines, and the movies. So sex isn't the big secret it used to be, whose mysteries were not to be revealed until you reached a certain age.

Nevertheless, a great many parents are just as embarrassed to talk about sex with their daughters as they used to be. Some even more so, since they are inclined to think that girls are growing up too soon these days, and that alarms and confuses them. And even though girls may know more about sex today than they used to, most of them are still embarrassed and reluctant to discuss the subject with their parents. "Oh, Mother!" is still their common response, which is designed to end the conversation.

I hope this book will help both you and your parents to build a bridge over the unnecessary gulf that separates you, if one does, so that you'll both be able to talk naturally about something that is certainly the most natural thing in the world, and surely the most common human activity. Young girls today have a potential sexual freedom that no previous generation ever enjoyed, but many of them aren't sure what to do with it, or about it, and parents are worried that they'll do the *wrong* thing. Yet the guidelines are simple enough. It's primarily a matter of knowledge and common sense, especially knowledge.

We're at a new stage in the evolution of our attitudes about sex. It's not the "sexual revolution" we've heard so much about. Some people persist in calling our changed attitudes "permissiveness," but they've been calling it that in one way or another for thousands of years. An Egyptian papyrus of 1700 B.C. tells us that the elders of an Egyptian city were convinced the young people of their community were going to the dogs, as the old saying goes. They complained about the disregard for authority by the young, and they were especially annoyed because young boys were driving their chariots recklessly over the landscape without regard for life or limb. As for the girls, the elders were horrified that they were shamelessly painting their lips with henna.

But if it seems that things haven't changed since then, that's only partly true. In fact, a steady process of evolution has gone on, and today we're at a major new stage in this process because of our changing perception of the role of women in our society. The fact that women now make up nearly half the work force, that they no longer have little choice but to stay home and keep house and raise children, that the doors to all kinds of careers are opening to them that were once closed—these and other factors of social change have given women an entirely new position. Some, it's true, prefer the old position, but the important fact is that freedom of choice is now possible.

As equality of the sexes becomes more of a social reality, we've seen a remarkable change in the old double standard about sex. My colleague, Dr. Kinsey, was the first to recognize that women have the same biological sexual response as men, and today more and more women have begun to understand their own sexuality a great deal better, to be more assertive about it, and to insist that they are sexual beings as much as men, with needs and desires of their own. The sexes are different in their psychological responses, but that's a matter we'll take up later.

If there's one kind of sexual activity that's still almost as divisive as it ever was, it's premarital sex. Generally, people accept the fact that there is now more of it at an earlier age, as far as actual intercourse is concerned, and that many people are now choosing to live together without getting married. As in other aspects of sex, women don't regard marriage as inevitable or absolutely required by society. They have choices. But even in accepting that much, most parents are still against premarital sex on the part of their teenage daughters, and even when they're a little older. It's common to hear mothers of college girls say, "Well, I know she's living with him off campus, but if she brings him home, she can't sleep with him—not under *my* roof." As for girls of high school age and under, not only does the law forbid it, but most parents don't approve of premarital intercourse even when they suspect it's occurring. Some parents, of course, are more strict than others in trying to prevent it.

Over the past forty or fifty years, there's been a gradual increase in the amount of premarital intercourse, particularly at upper social levels. We can see it in the rate of teenage pregnancies—which is especially ironic because contraceptives are so much more easily available. That teenage intercourse can also bring its problems is evident in the high suicide rate among teens, although much of that may be more related to young people's despair over the chaotic world they find themselves in rather than to their personal sex-related difficulties.

4

The key word, however, is still "acceptance." Even at lower social levels today there is more acceptance, not only of premarital intercourse, but of masturbation, nudity, and variety in petting and coital techniques than in the past. All this is reflected in the treatment of sex by the media. It's hard to believe that the word "syphilis" never appeared in an American newspaper until 1932, and that it was four years later before the word was uttered on the radio. The word "masturbation" wasn't seen in a newspaper in this country until 1948, and homosexuality wasn't discussed in the mass media until about 1960. Now it's difficult to find newspapers, books, magazines, or plays that *don't* deal with these subjects in one way or another, openly and more or less freely, although often with much ignorance.

Does all this mean that there's been an equal change in overt sexual *behavior*? Probably not. It simply means that there has been a change in the open *discussion* of sex. We're a very big country now, more than 220 million of us, and because of the increase in our population, there are more people engaging in sexual behavior of all sorts, which leads to the erroneous conclusion that there's been an increase in sexual activity.

Another change we've seen is in the status of pornography, once condemned by law as well as by people. Many people still do condemn it, and militant feminists have opposed it on grounds that it degrades women. But the Supreme Court, after years of trying to define it, has been sufficiently vague in its recent decisions so that almost anything can now be printed, or seen in stationary or moving images. We haven't seen the last of this argument by any means; there are strong forces in the nation that want a return to the old restrictions, but for now, we have the freedom that the First Amendment has guaranteed all along.

If our society is really heading toward still more liberal attitudes about sex, there's a question—and it especially arises among parents—as to what the effect of it will be. You've undoubtedly heard older people predict that the result will be the downfall of civilization, and no doubt they will cite the Romans. Yet there is no classical scholar who believes that the sexual habits of the Romans led to the fall of their civilization.

On the other hand, there is no reason to believe that even greater sexual freedom will mean a new era of universal happiness and self-fulfillment. It won't, if it happens, decrease racial tension and war, improve the lot of the poor, or lead us directly into healthier, happier lives.

Both the pessimists and the optimists are wrong about one thing. Sexuality is not the primary moving force in human experience, as they seem to think it is, and encouraging or discouraging it won't resolve all our problems. Sexual experience is more an effect than a cause. As we all know, sexual intercourse itself can be a deeply emotional and loving experience, but it can also be an aggressive and hostile act or no more than a casual toss on the mattress. And the same thing can be said for any other kind of sexual behavior.

The fact is that we really don't know as much as we think we do about sex. We're still in the Dark Ages as far as solid research data on sexual behavior is concerned. Fewer than a hundred research projects in this field could be said to be adequate and important. No other area of human behavior remains so unexplored.

Nevertheless, the inadequacy of our knowledge doesn't mean that boys and girls, as well as their parents, don't have a responsibility to know as much as they can about sex, or that they shouldn't make as much sense out of it as possible. Parents, especially, should stop viewing sexual behavior through the distorted lenses of their inherited prejudices, and see it as part of a changing world in which their children need to grow up to be useful and reasonably happy citizens.

But daughters, as I've indicated, have a particularly hard time in getting this kind of viewpoint from their parents. Traditionally, young girls have occupied a protected position in society, and even parents who talk easily about the changing role of sex in society are likely to be much less accepting when it comes to the behavior of their own daughters.

Things change slowly. Parents still ask me, "How can I talk to my daughter about sex?" They still seem to feel, by and large, that if such talk takes place at all it's a matter between mother and daughter. The ques-

7

tion usually arises when a girl is seen to be growing up, as so many of them do these days at an early age, and especially when they start wanting to go out on dates.

However, I tell parents that when they raise the question at that age, they're raising it about ten years too late. "In the first place," I say, "you've been communicating with your daughter about sex from the time she was old enough to understand anything. *Not* talking with her about sex is communicating with her about it. Not talking is telling your daughter that this is a taboo topic that is not to be discussed and must therefore be something special, secret, fearful, and bad. Because you have instilled these feelings in your daughter by not talking about sex," I go on, "she in turn will not open the subject herself, nor will she come to you with her questions about it."

Parents say to me so many times, "But my daughter is so young and innocent. She needs protection from all the ugliness and misery sex may produce in later life." But do we really protect children by keeping them in a state of ignorance—even if we could? Every sex therapist knows that ignorance is at the root of much sex-connected ugliness and misery.

As a teenage girl, you may well have your own difficulties in talking about sex with your parents, but you're learning every day just the same, in school and elsewhere. Your feelings about a teacher may be telling you something. Your feelings about a particular boy, good or bad, may not seem sexual at the time,

8

but they could well be a cover-up for a beginning sexual interest in him.

What you read in newspapers offers an opportunity for you and your parents to discuss sexual matters. No newspaper is without stories involving sex, because it is so often news. Articles about contraception and population control, adultery, illegitimacy, child molesting, rape, and other offenses against the law provide opportunities to put into perspective what might otherwise be frightening or mystifying to you. Other topics —censorship of books or movies, war and its effects on people's sex lives—provide other openings. Even a story pointing out that good nutrition corresponds highly with early puberty could be an opportunity for discussion.

I hope the parents who read this will remember something that you and most other adolescents are always saying: "Don't preach, don't lecture." Talking about sex should be a calm, objective exchange of feelings and information and views, without making a point of it.

Parents are often afraid to bring up sexual topics because they're afraid it will stimulate a child's interest in sex and that talking about it will lead to experimenting—as though interest and experimentation weren't going to happen anyway. Besides, children who are baffled and ignorant about sex are all the more likely to try to find out. In any case, children are going to explore their own bodies and those of their playmates, and although that may frighten some parents, there's no evidence that any harm is done.

So the question is not *what* girls do sexually, but how they *feel* about what they do, and what kinds of relationships they develop with other people. These are the factors that determine what kind of human beings they turn out to be.

There are a few differences between boys and girls that affect their attitudes and sexual behavior with each other. One of the most striking differences is that boys are more oriented toward their genitals, generally speaking, and are somewhat more concerned with genital activity. A girl is more concerned with the things surrounding sex than with sex itself. If boys and girls understood this simple fact better, they'd be better able to get along with each other.

Another difference is the greater concern the girl has for her reputation, not only where her peers are concerned, but also with the adult world, although this traditional difference also seems to be changing. Parents have helped to create that difference, and the damage it does is that girls may determine what they do or don't do mostly on the basis of what other people may think about them, rather than on what their true feelings may be. But in the new climate in which girls and women live today, even these standards are rapidly falling. Girls used to be taught to be "ladylike," that is, feminine, demure, nonaggressive, dresses down and legs crossed, told not to "chase the boys." These ideas are being rapidly replaced. Girls understand now that they are far more likely to make good social and sexual adjustments to life if they learn to be warm, open, responsive, and sexually unafraid. They're learning to be sexual *partners* of men, with equal needs, responses, and responsibilities, not possessions of men.

Some girls are lucky enough to learn all this from their mothers as role models; some are not. Those mothers who are openly affectionate, warm, and loving toward both their daughters and their husbands are more likely to have happy and well-adjusted girls in their families. It is right to be as open, relaxed, and objective about sex as it is possible to be. Parents who find it hard to be so need to review their own sex lives and ask themselves whether they've been so free of guilt and fear that they've never had any problems.

Let me say again that knowledge is the most important element. In the pages that follow, I've tried to supply the latest and most reliable information about the sex lives of girls in a way they'll understand, one that will help them to fulfill their roles in this complicated world.

CHAPTER 1
A Girl's Sex Life

If you're a girl growing up today, you may feel that you already know quite a lot about sex. That may be true, but whether what you know is correct is another matter. I suspect many of you would like to know a great deal more than you do, but don't know where to go to find specific answers about sex and to hear a point of view that isn't moralistic or "preachy." To provide such information is the reason this book came into being, just as did *Boys and Sex*, the similar volume I've written for boys. Experience has shown that both sexes read and profit from each other's books.

But I had another reason for writing these books. I want to show what results can be expected from different kinds of sexual behavior, and the meaning that such behavior can have for different individuals. "Meaning," of course, isn't the same for everyone. Sex means different things to different people. For some it means only reproduction. To others it means behavior, like the changes in the body that occur when someone is sexually aroused. These changes can be the result of various kinds of psychological stimulation, or they can result from stimulation by the individual herself or by some other person.

Then there are people who have a much broader idea of sex. To them, for instance, it may have to do with how a girl acts and feels simply because she is a girl, and with what her role is in our society. Volumes could be written about this way of looking at sex, and many have been. I'll have a few things to say about that in this book, but mostly I'm going to confine myself to sex as a specific kind of behavior and talk about what meaning that behavior might have for a teenage girl.

Some parents and other adults believe teenage girls aren't ready for much information about sex at that stage of their lives, and probably more of these people, with traditional attitudes, will be upset by this book than they would be by the book for boys. That's natural, since girls have until recently been much more protected in our society. For my part, however, I believe that if people are going to have sex relations with each other, or even contemplate having them, both need an equal amount of information, and it's unfair to put girls at a disadvantage by "protecting" them.

Before they begin reading the information that follows, however, girls may want to know what *my* attitudes are. Let me say first that I believe what we need most is *understanding* of sex by both girls and boys, so that they will find fulfillment and happiness in each other. The key to understanding is that word we're all so familiar with these days—communication. Girls and boys, men and women, need to learn to communicate with each other, which means being honest and open, not afraid to let the other person know how we feel, especially in sexual matters. Sex itself is one of the most important ways people communicate with each other. Sometimes that communication can be a great experience, but it can also be negative when it becomes hostile or hurtful.

That's why I said earlier in this chapter that girls (and boys) who think they know a lot about sex may not know as much as they imagine. It's a very complex matter, not the simple one so many people believe it is, and that's why it's been written about and discussed for centuries at such extraordinary length.

We know that sex is an important factor in everyone's life, but even professionals in sex psychology are not agreed about its role in teenage life. Some say sexual intercourse is only for adults and they don't think young teenagers are able to handle it. They want reasonable limits to be set, meaning that girls and boys should feel free to experiment sexually, which they're going to do anyway, but shouldn't go beyond petting to orgasm. Others advocate more freedom, and some less.

I think everyone's agreed, however, that teenage sex should be a learning experience, and not a frightening one, and that setting certain limits may make it less likely to be frightening, particularly for young girls. The question of whether a girl should engage in any kind of sexual behavior depends on the attitude of the people with whom she lives, especially those of her own age; the particular social level on which she lives (the problems of inner city children and those in the suburbs are not always the same); and whatever system of values, ethics, codes, or religion she has chosen to guide her. In any case, I believe that whatever a girl decides about sex should be based on as much information as possible, of the kind I want to provide here. I intend to give girls as much information about sex in this book as I can.

I have some other convictions, too. I believe that in the past we've put far too much emphasis in our society on the question of intercourse before marriage. With the change in our climate of acceptance, it's much clearer now that what is important is the relationship between two people. How they feel about each other is what is important, not whether a penis enters a vagina.

My feeling is that sexual behavior for both boys and girls is something that's pleasurable and desirable, as long as certain rules are followed. The rules are simple:

1. Don't do anything to hurt someone else or go against his wishes and desires—in short, be responsible toward the other person.

2. Whatever is done, do it so that it won't get the other person into trouble.

I also respect those who choose not to engage in any sexual experiences. That's their right.

These are my attitudes, then, and I'm sure you've already begun to agree or disagree. What I hope, though, is that you'll begin to examine more closely what your *own* attitudes are about sex, why you feel the way you do, or why you may not be exactly clear about *how* you feel.

To begin finding a path out of whatever confusion may exist, a path that's yours alone, think for a minute about the real differences between boys and girls. It isn't just the obvious difference in anatomy. It's the way the two sexes approach life, the roles they play in society and in their sexual lives. As I've observed earlier, the present generation of girls is in a different position from the ones that preceded them, because their role is undergoing a major change, with a good deal of confusion attending it, and many of the traditional differences between the sexes are now disappearing in the new climate.

We've come to understand, as I've said, that girls have sexual needs similar to boys', and that the rapid move toward equality of the sexes has also accelerated the departure of the double standard that has prevailed for so long. Still, when all of that has been recognized, there are differences that remain, and it's important to understand them. It's hard for adults as well as teenagers to understand sex, but in our increasingly complex world, we need to try, because sex difficulties are a factor, even though they may not be the chief one, in a great many divorces, and for those who stay married, sex problems often bring them to the doctor, the clergyman, the marriage counselor, or some other kind of therapist.

Let's examine a few of the real differences between the sexes. To boys, sex is often an awareness of changes in their bodies—physical changes that happen when they're sexually aroused. That may happen when they see pictures, read books, hear stories, think of sexy situations, touch persons of the opposite sex or even the same sex, or if they touch their own bodies. Arousal means that the blood rushes to the surface of the skin and makes it warm; the penis hardens and becomes erect, increasing in size from about three and a half to six inches; the breath comes faster. These things can happen every day of their lives, and usually do.

Girls are often unaware that this is what's happening to boys, and don't know that it can even be a source of embarrassment to them, especially when they have to stand up in class and discover that they have an erection. Boys are upset to think that others will see the bulge in their pants they can't conceal. When a boy dates a girl, sometimes the awkwardness and shyness he exhibits only means he's fighting against the sexual response he feels. Even though the girl is usually completely unaware of it, the boy would be deeply embarrassed if he thought she knew.

When *they're* aroused, girls go through the same kind of bodily changes boys do—that is, they feel warm and flushed and their breath comes faster. Instead of the erection, they feel dampness in their genitals because of the lubrication of the vagina that has taken place. Girls who haven't been aroused very much may be surprised if they find out other girls have had such sensations.

In both boys and girls, if this kind of stimulation continues, it will increase in intensity until a pitch of excitement is reached that is nearly uncontrollable. At this point there is sometimes a sudden release of sexual tension, followed by a quiet, relaxed, blissful feeling. This discharge of tension is what we call "orgasm," or sexual climax. It happens sometimes during petting, or during intercourse, or when a girl or a boy rubs his or her own sex organ, or it may happen at night while dreaming about sex.

Girls who understand why their response to sexual stimulation is not the same as it is for boys, even though physically the reaction may be much the same, can see why it is that boys are able to feel more at home with sex. It's simply because it's so much a part of their lives. Girls have sexual needs and desires too, and respond when they're aroused, but they're still taught restraint where sex is concerned, even though times are changing these roles. They're still conditioned not to "pursue" boys, and parents usually want them to come home from a date at whatever they think is a reasonable time, for obvious reasons. These restrictions often irritate girls and cause friction at home, but in the end, as far as actual behavior is concerned, it's their own decision about when they feel mature enough to handle sexual situations with boys. The old idea that a girl suddenly became a sexual being when she got married is not believed any more by most young girls. They may not want to marry at all, or at least intend to defer it to some indefinite time in the future, and meanwhile they expect to experience their own sexuality—but at their own time and at their own pace.

For boys, arousal and erection are the beginning of a drive toward orgasm, and they are quite as ready to achieve it with a girl at a young age as a later one, if they have the opportunity. We can see this fundamental difference in the fact that, by the time they're fifteen, nearly all boys are having orgasm, on the average of two or three times a week. For two thirds of them, their first orgasm comes from masturbation; for one fifth, from sexual dreams; and for less than one sixth, from petting. Less than one in ten has had it from intercourse. Most boys continue to have orgasm as a result of masturbation.

On the other hand, only about half of the girls have been aroused at all by any means by the time they're fifteen, although there are indications that this percentage is changing since the time Kinsey measured it. In the next five years, however, their lives change rapidly. By the time they're twenty, about nine out of ten have experienced some kind of arousal. Yet at fifteen, only a fourth of them have experienced orgasm from any source, and five years later, the figure is no more than half. About a third are aroused by masturbation, a third by petting, and another third through psychological stimulation from books, pictures, fantasies, dreams, or whatever. Two fifths of the girls experience their first orgasm from masturbation, one in twenty from dreams, a fourth from petting, one in ten from premarital intercourse, a surprising one in six from marital intercourse, and three percent from homosexual contacts.

The boys who are having orgasm at fifteen, which includes nearly all of them, are having it two or three times a week, as I've said, and they are dating girls of the same age, three fourths of whom are not having any orgasm at all and the other fourth only once every two weeks. It's no wonder there's trouble when people with such widely different sex experience get together on dates. It's easy to see why there's so much misunderstanding.

It's a fact that males are sexually mature and active at thirteen or earlier, while girls develop sexually more slowly, in spite of the fact that they are becoming biologically ready for sex at increasingly earlier times. But a boy is at his sexual peak during adolescence and then becomes gradually less active as he grows older, although some men remain sexually active until they are in their nineties. Women, however, developing more gradually, reach a peak of responsiveness in their thirties, forties, or even fifties. And their response is not only as great as that of men, but can be greater. Consequently, the troubles caused by the differences of adolescence go right on into adult life, and aren't easily solved unless there's real understanding on both sides.

There are also important sexual differences among girls themselves, and it seems hard for people to understand that there's a wide range of sexual interest and responsiveness among them. Boys, especially, usually have no idea that there are many girls who are simply uninterested in sex itself, and who are not sexually aroused by pictures, books, or by what they see in the movies. They're not necessarily apathetic about boys, however. They may like boys and want to date them and enjoy their company, but sex hasn't yet become a part of their conscious lives.

At the other extreme are a small number of girls who are more easily aroused than boys by seeing, reading, and thinking of sexual things. They have orgasm frequently, quickly, and easily, and often undergo a real struggle to keep out of trouble in a society that doesn't always approve of such behavior. They may also have difficulty in their own teenage society if most of the other girls are not as uninhibited, which is usually the case.

Another large class of girls falls in the middle ground between these extremes, but it's a fact that most are far closer to the "unresponsive" end of the scale than to the uninhibited end. This is particularly true of girls between the ages of thirteen and seventeen.

With all these differences among themselves and between themselves and boys, girls often find it hard to adjust to the world they live in. Society seems still to want them to behave in a certain way and live within certain rules laid down by the community in general, yet they're encouraged by what's going on around them to behave differently. The wide range of differences among them that I've just described are not taken into account, and they're all lumped together as "girls," just as they will later be categorized by many people as "women," without regard for differences.

If a girl gives in to a boy sexually, she steps out of the role society has assigned to her at that age, and both she and the boy may wind up being confused about what's happened to them. Unless a girl rejects society completely, she can expect that the penalties will be what they've always been, more or less, if what she's doing becomes known to her parents or in some cases even to her peers. It's no wonder that girls are so often confused when they see permissiveness all around them and yet are subjected to the social pressures put on them by parents and other members of the adult community. Sometimes they don't know where to turn or how to behave.

Since that's the case, it may be fortunate that sex isn't as much of a problem to girls as it is to boys, by and large, nor even as much a problem as their parents may think it is. Sex is less important to girls than their public image. Boys, by contrast, are not so concerned about their sexual reputation and may even be proud to be considered "studs." But girls are often painfully conscious of what other people think of them, and

especially what other girls think. In spite of the freedom they have today, they're still fearful of getting a
bad reputation, or of being known as easy marks for
boys who want sex, or of being outside the accepted
social pattern.

Girls seldom talk about sex as sex, and even when
they do, they don't talk about it as boys do. Boys
talk about sex a lot; they constantly trade information
about it or make jokes about it, even though much of
what they think they know may be wrong. Girls' conversation, on the other hand, as far as social matters
are concerned, centers on dates and clothes and the
personalities of individual boys, not on their probable
availability for sex or on specific sexual activities.
Their view of sex is more romantic, which is something boys ought to know and remember.

When a girl is asked, "Do you have any sex dreams
at night?" she'll often answer, "Yes," and if she's asked
about the content of the dreams, the response will
show quite clearly the difference between what girls
and boys mean when they say "sex." The girl will say
she dreamed about being with a boy somewhere, having
fun with him that isn't necessarily sexual. If she says
she dreamed of making love with a boy, further ques-
tioning often discloses that what she means is that it
wasn't intercourse or perhaps even petting, but some
dreamlike, warm, affectionate relationship with a boy
she likes.

This romantic, affectionate feeling is what a girl

usually dreams about, awake as well as asleep, rather than some particular kind of sexual behavior. Her night dreams and daytime fantasies are quite different from what boys are experiencing. A boy will dream or fantasize a specific, step-by-step description of a petting session with a girl, letting himself imagine in detail the experiencing of one sexual sensation after another. Girls are rarely so specific. For a girl, the fantasy, the dream, is usually a full moon, a cool breeze, a warm and happy feeling of being with a boy.

Girls might understand themselves better where sex is concerned if they could talk with their parents, but that's no more possible for them in most cases than it is for the boys. There isn't much exchange between the generations on this point. And for the girls, embarrassment on the part of the parents is likely to be a greater problem than it is for the boys. Fathers, especially, find it difficult because they so often have such intense fears of their daughters' being involved sexually with boys. Partly that's because they're afraid a girl may get pregnant, but it's also partly due to their common reluctance to accept the fact that their daughters are maturing. In the normal course of events, fathers are jealous of this maturing and don't want to relinquish their daughters to boys, who are seen subconsciously as male rivals.

As for the mothers, they've lived through this adolescent period themselves and struggle with the same problems as their daughters—when to begin to experience sex with a boy, lack of real knowledge about sex, and all the other anxieties. Now they relive this period of uncertainty through their daughters. Naturally, they reflect and re-create whatever it was they experienced.

Knowing these facts about parents won't necessarily solve the daughter-parent dilemma for most girls, but the knowledge may help them to understand what may often seem to them unreasonable attitudes on the part of their parents.

What other facts should a girl know about sex as she grows up and lives through this difficult period of her life—that is, after she's absorbed the fundamental differences between herself and boys?

I believe she ought to know something about the anatomy of the sexual parts of her own body and about that of boys. She needs to understand what causes the changes in her body when she's aroused sexually, as I described earlier. She ought to have some insight into her early sexual experiences and understand what effect they may have on her later life. It's also helpful to have more information about her *social* relations with boys, as in dating, and even more specifically, about her *sexual* relations with boys, as in petting—if you'll forigve me for using the old word for sexual activity that stops short of intercourse; no one seems to have invented an adequate substitute for it.

I also think it will be helpful for a girl to know what intercourse is like and to understand the pros and cons of when she should learn to experience it—at what age she's ready, in an emotional sense, for sex. Few girls these days wait until marriage to have intercourse. Then, too, I think it's important for a girl to get more information about the stimulation of her own body and to have a better understanding of the meaning of sexual relations between members of the same sex. Especially, she needs to know the difference between boys and girls when it comes to sexual behavior and attitudes, in the ways I've described. That will determine how well she's going to make a sexual adjustment either in marriage or some other intimate relationship.

Armed with all this knowledge, I'm convinced a girl will come to understand that she must be something of an actress in life. It will be clear to her that she's been given three roles to play. One is her role in society, first as a young girl growing up, then as a wife and mother, or as a career girl or a combination of both, whatever the case may be. The second role is her relationship with boys, in which she has to learn to adjust to social roles and at the same time develop her own sexuality. The third role is perhaps the most difficult—the role she must play as herself, an individual responsible to herself.

No actress in the theater or the movies could have a more difficult combination of roles. As an adolescent, a girl is engaged in learning how to adjust to society, to the adult world. Yet she must get along with boys, who may have the same expectations of her as the adult world does and at the same time regard her as a sexual object. And yet, in spite of all this, a girl has her own self, her own feelings, to consider. It isn't easy.

I hope the information in this book will truly help girls to play their triple role in a way that will bring them into the adult world with the best prospects for happiness.

CHAPTER 2
The Body and Sex

In girls, as in boys, changes develop as they approach puberty and pass through it into adolescence. There are changes in body size and shape, in the breasts and the sex organs. Menstruation begins, and after that it's possible for girls to conceive and bear children.

Usually the changes begin about the time a girl is twelve years old, but there's no hard-and-fast rule about that. Sometimes it's earlier, sometimes later, and the average age has been slowly dropping over the past few decades. Some girls have pubic hair and developing breasts when they're as young as eight or nine, while others don't exhibit these signs until they're fifteen or older. The reasons for these wide variations are not entirely known, but one is undoubtedly the inheritance a girl has from her parents, making her predisposed to develop early or late. Nutrition is another factor. Girls with better nutrition develop earlier, while those who don't eat properly as they grow up tend to develop later.

Even though it makes no difference in a sexual sense whether a girl develops earlier or later, it does matter to her socially. Every girl (and the same is true for

boys) gets some sense of well-being from the knowledge that she is like the people around her, and so the
early and late developers feel themselves to be different
from their friends—the very tall or the very short girl,
for instance—and may be uncomfortable about it.
These differences may affect a girl's social outlook,
but if we're talking only about sex development, there's
some consolation in the fact that, either way, the
others will be like her eventually, or she will be like
them.

Probably the part of their body development that
girls worry about most is the breasts. Unfair though
it may be, they're soon aware that they will be more
attractive to boys as their breasts develop, but they're
often bothered and made unhappy, with good reason,
by the emphasis that seems to be placed on these
glands. Adolescent girls are inclined to worry a great
deal, needlessly, about their breasts, mostly because
they think them too small. A few are concerned over
whether they're too large, and some worry because
they think their breasts are developing unevenly. But
the fact is that breasts, like other parts of the anatomy,
come in all sizes and appear to be attached to the
body in a variety of ways. It's possible for plastic
surgeons to increase and decrease the size of breasts,
but girls soon realize as they grow up that size isn't
important, as they thought it was at the beginning of
puberty.

Much of the trouble, of course, comes from the
preoccupation with breasts that has become so much

a part of American culture in this century (although it exists in other cultures as well and historically extends to other centuries). Girls with large breasts have been held up as objects of sexual admiration in advertising, in motion pictures, and in a hundred other ways. All this makes girls with small breasts feel inferior and fearful that boys won't like them.

Nothing could be further from the truth. In the first place, few girls (or women) are built like movie stars, yet they have no trouble finding boys to love them and marry them, even if they have small breasts. Even before the women's movement made a point of it, it was true that there are far more important things about a girl that interest boys than the size of these glands. Just the same, girls with small breasts might want to know that breasts become larger during sexual arousal, sometimes by as much as 25 percent. In any event, you may be sure that boys are going to like you for yourself, not because of the size of your brassiere.

Girls who are preoccupied about the growth of their breasts don't take the time to know and understand the rest of their anatomy. It's amazing but true that girls rarely examine their own sex organs to see how they're put together. Of course, it's a little more difficult for them than for boys, whose organs are visible and accessible, and it's universally true of males that they examine their own penises and scrotums. But if girls had a little more curiosity, it would repay them in many ways to hold a small mirror in one hand and part their pubic hair with the other. If they did, they would understand their own anatomy considerably better.

What they would see first is a primary difference between the sexes—that girls have one more body opening than boys. Both have the anus, through which the body's solid waste materials are excreted, but there the resemblance ends. The boy has one other opening, at the end of the penis, through which he discharges his urine and the sperm-laden fluid of his ejaculation. But the girl has a special opening to discharge the urine and a third opening besides, between the urinary outlet (the urethra) and the anus. This is called the vagina. She also has, near the top of the vulva—the collective term doctors use for all those organs visible outside the body—a tiny penislike organ called the clitoris. This small organ has a rich supply of nerve endings, and when it's stimulated, it provides sexual pleasure. The vulva includes two folds of skin —an outer one, the "labia majora," and an inner one, the "labia minora."

The vagina is a passageway between the external vulva and the internal sex organs, which include the uterus (or womb), the ovaries, and the Fallopian tubes, all of these encased within the protective framework of the pelvis, that part of the abdominal cavity which lies between the hipbones.

In every way the vagina is a remarkable organ. Its walls possess an astonishing flexibility. A penis, no matter how large, will not test the capacity of the vagina, because its walls can stretch and stretch to permit the passage of a baby in birth—a truly remarkable thing when we remember that, on the average, the vagina is only three to three and a half inches long. It is an organ of many uses, designed to provide a canal for the menstrual flow, to receive the penis in intercourse, to hold the sperm cells when the male has discharged them and start them on their journey upward; and it provides the pathway for a baby's birth.

The vagina is lubricated a little by fluid from glands in the cervix, to which it is attached at the upper end, and a little more by other glands located near the outer opening. But mostly it is lubricated by internal secretions from its own walls—like sweat on the body —when these walls get warm in response to sexual stimulation. A girl will feel these secretions—"feel wet" around the vulva and possibly on her thighs— when she is sexually aroused.

Over the entrance to the vagina is a thin membrane called the hymen, with an opening in it. This opening allows menstrual fluid to pass through, and the hymen is pliable enough so that a tampon can be inserted. Girls used to worry that when they had their first intercourse and the hymen was broken, they would feel pain and would bleed. In reality, the "pain" is usually no more than a brief twinge, and the blood a mere trickle when it occurs, and it doesn't always occur. In any case, hymens are very often broken before first intercourse these days since women exercise a great deal more actively than they used to in all kinds of sports. Hymens are sometimes broken, too, when girls masturbate by putting a finger or some other object in the vagina. Often the hymen breaks so easily a girl doesn't even know when it happens. Only rarely is the membrane so tough that it requires a doctor to break it.

A girl is usually first conscious of her sex organs at adolescence, when she begins to menstruate. That usually happens about a year after the appearance of pubic hair and the beginning of breast development. But again there is considerable variation among girls, and it may not happen precisely at that time. There's no reason to worry, however, if menstruation doesn't occur until later. As with other symptoms of sexual development, whether it's early or late has no particular meaning.

Some girls feel bad about the adolescent change in their bodies because life becomes different from what they've been accustomed to for so long. Others don't like the idea of growing up. In either case, they're likely to think that menstruation is a messy business, and if they happen to have cramps, aches, and pains, as some do, they resent this intrusion into their well-being every month. And then when they realize that it's something that's going to happen to them for the next twenty-five to forty years, a few girls are seized with a kind of despair, feeling themselves trapped. Most girls, however, take a different view of it. They are pleased by the onset of menstruation because they *do* want to grow up, and they understand that this is one of the most important parts of that process. Menstruation means becoming a woman.

Menstruation can also be a happier beginning when there's an understanding parent involved. I knew of one father who observed the occasion of his daughter's first menstruation by bringing her flowers and making a little ceremony of the fact that now she had become a young woman. That daughter couldn't help feeling proud and good about becoming adolescent.

Still, for many girls, menstruation comes as a dismaying shock. Since there is so little communication between parents and children about sex, these girls are unprepared for it. When it does begin, most mothers instruct their daughters what to do about it and inform them that it will be with them most of their lives. But they usually give the girls precious little information about what's actually happening to them.

There isn't anything at all mysterious about it. What has happened inside the girl's body is that her ovaries have begun to function. These organs, one on each side of the uterus, carry the eggs that create another life when they are combined with a male sperm. In most instances, one of these eggs matures every month, and about halfway between periods of menstruation it breaks loose from the follicle that encloses it in the ovary and moves down into the Fallopian tube. This follicle is only a covering for the egg, but it also has the function of producing the female sex hormone, estrogen. This hormone provides a girl with the characteristics identifying her as female, and the companion ovarian hormone, progesterone, also prepares the uterine lining for pregnancy, if the egg is fertilized by the sperm.

The follicle, after the egg has left it, changes color and becomes something else, called "the yellow body." It is larger now and begins to affect the lining of the uterus, providing it with blood pools concentrated under the cell layers, so that the baby will have oxygen and food if conception occurs.

But if fertilization doesn't take place, the whole scene changes. The egg simply disintegrates in a few hours and is gone. The yellow body disappears, too, since it no longer has any purpose. What remains are the blood pools it created, but since the body is not equipped to take these back into the circulatory system, the blood and the cell layers in the lining of the uterus slip out through the vagina. That's what we call "menstruation." Girls who are afraid because they think they're passing so much blood should know that they're losing only about one to three ounces of it. Nor is this menstrual blood like the blood that spurts out when you cut yourself, because it is mixed with the mucous membrane from the womb. A girl should not feel squeamish about it, as some do. Actually, people frequently have intercourse during menstruation and feel entirely comfortable about it.

If menstruation is irregular when it first begins, there's no reason to worry about it. Several months sometimes elapse between the first and second time, and irregularity is perfectly natural among young girls. It only means that the ovaries haven't begun producing mature eggs on a regular basis. There's no reason, either, to worry about the length of the period. Sometimes it takes only three days, sometimes as much as seven. Five days would be the average, but a girl might not always menstruate for the same number of days.

Another variation in the process is the way menstruation affects a girl mentally and physically. Some girls have their period regularly, have no forewarning until it begins, and no symptoms of any kind, except perhaps a feeling of fullness. Others not only have a common symptom, cramps, but they feel depressed and vaguely unhappy; their bodies seem heavy and lumpy, and they are listless and tired for a day or two. A combination of psychological and physical factors, like congestion, may produce this feeling. Aspirin and a little mild exercise are the best remedies. The only danger is that a girl will take her symptoms so seriously that she will use menstruation as an excuse to retreat from life into illness every month, to gain attention, or to avoid some real-life situation.

There is no need for a girl to feel crippled or "out of the running" when she's menstruating. If she does, she should see her doctor. She can do nearly everything she's accustomed to doing, except that it's probably a good idea not to exercise too violently on the first day. But it's only a superstition that a girl can't take a bath or a shower or go in swimming or wash her hair when she menstruates. The only thing she needs to be a little careful of is to avoid getting chilled, because her body is more susceptible to chilling at that particular time. A healthy girl can exercise, go to classes, work, go to parties, or do anything else she likes while she menstruates. She'll feel better if she gets enough sleep and if she takes in more fluids than usual, like fruit juice and milk, and avoids rich, starchy foods. But then, that's good advice in general.

One thing that bothers some girls is the odor of menstruation and the increased activity of the sweat glands. That's easily counteracted by paying attention to personal hygiene, using deodorants under the arms and on the sanitary pads. Pads or tampons should be changed frequently.

Some girls like pads, others prefer tampons. Many use pads the first day or two, then switch. The choice is personal. There may well be, in my opinion, a good psychological reason for using tampons, however, because they teach a girl what it's like to have something in her vagina, and possibly that will make her feel more comfortable when she has intercourse for the first time. Sometimes a girl needs to be taught how to insert them properly. They shouldn't be forced in. Often it's helpful to lubricate the tip of the tampon before insertion. Even with minimal flow, they should be changed every four hours. Incidentally, there's no truth in the notion that using tampons will cause cancer.

Menstruation isn't the only kind of discharge to

come from the vagina. Sometimes there will be a slight bloody staining between periods, but that's nothing to worry about. It may happen as the egg leaves the ovary and moves down into the uterus. A girl may even feel a little brief pain on one side or the other. But that isn't true of all girls, or women, and those who experience it may have it for a half hour to a day. If, however, there is genuine bleeding between periods, much thicker and darker than the staining, or if the periods are very difficult, a girl should consult her doctor at once, because such bleeding is not normal and the difficulty may require medical attention.

Another kind of vaginal discharge that may occur is a seepage of fluid ranging in color from white to yellow, and often with a noticeable odor and with some itching or burning. This is sometimes caused by a fungus growth resulting from germs that have found their way into the vagina. It should have the attention of a doctor, who can cure it easily with medication. Girls ought not to feel so embarrassed about it that they won't even tell their mothers. If they do nothing, the infection may continue for some time. They should remember that it's no more special than a minor infection anywhere else in the body. The best advice is, tell your mother and get it taken care of promptly by the doctor.

Now let's see what happens when the vagina is penetrated by a male penis in intercourse and pregnancy results. Surprisingly, even in our era of freedom, this process is not really understood by many girls.

And it isn't such a simple cause-and-effect relationship as it may seem. When the male ejaculates, he pours his semen into the vagina. This semen contains millions of sperm cells, whose long tails begin to lash, moving them forward until they enter the cervix, which is the passageway into the uterus, or womb. The uterus is pear-shaped, looking a little like the head of a very small bull. Its "horns" are the Fallopian tubes, connecting the uterus with the ovaries. The sperm swim from the cervix into the uterus and up through these "horns." There they may or may not encounter an unfertilized egg cell coming down from an ovary on the once-a-month descent through the tubes.

If the sperm encounter an egg in the tubes, a bombardment of it results as the tiny sperm cells, lashing their tails, surround it and try to penetrate it. Pregnancy occurs when a sperm cell enters through the egg wall and merges with the egg, after which the cell wall immediately hardens up so that no more sperm can get in. The sperm cell that did the fertilizing becomes a part of the egg's nucleus. The other sperm die in a few hours. This whole process, from ejaculation to the encounter with the egg cell, may take as long as eight hours.

When sperm and egg join, fertilization takes place, and the baby is conceived at that moment. Sperm carrying Y chromosomes make boys; those with X chromosomes make girls. Sex is determined by whichever kind of sperm cell fertilizes the egg cell, and this is a matter of pure chance. Chance, in fact, is a large part of the whole process. The sperm must be in the Fallopian tubes at a time when the egg is traveling through it. It must be a vigorous sperm and the egg must be ripe. A woman produces only about 400 ripe eggs in her entire lifetime, and there are only about twelve to twenty-four hours in every month when it's possible for a ripe egg to be fertilized.

If these odds against pregnancy encourage a girl and a boy to "take a chance," they should remember that sexual Russian roulette is a dangerous game, and in the end, the odds are against them and the risk is far too great.

Just as there are many misconceptions about getting pregnant, there are probably nearly as many about childbirth. Girls sometimes hear so many horror stories about the agony of birth and the distress of pregnancy itself that they are badly frightened of getting pregnant even when they are married, and, if they do, live in a state of fear until the baby comes.

We've gone a long way in overcoming these fears. Many women now practice so-called "natural child-birth," meaning that they're taught to give birth without the aid of anesthetics or any kind of pain killer, learning to take part in the process in an active way so that they can participate in the experience. Often men are drawn into the natural birth too, as husbands go into the delivery room and share with their wives what's happening, making it more meaningful for both of them.

Girls who worry about how something as large as a

baby could come out of anything as small as a vagina should remember the incredible stretching capacity of that organ. It's the stretching of the cervix that hurts, but many women have learned to have little fear or pain by learning the techniques of natural childbirth.

For those who find themselves unable to accept these techniques, modern anesthetics can help to decrease the pain. In any case, there is little danger in properly supervised childbirth these days. For one thing, women see their doctor regularly during pregnancy, and he (or she) is consequently able to anticipate any possible complication. While it's true that complications may occur, the chances of their happening are extremely low. As for those that can occur during the last three months, the odds are about one in two hundred that they'll ever happen, and even then doctor and patient, working together, can either prevent any trouble or take care of it properly as soon as it happens.

Whatever discomfort is involved during pregnancy or birth is more than made up for, as millions of women can testify, by the special joy of giving birth to a baby.

This, then, is the cycle of change in a girl from the time of her beginning adolescence until she has her first child. Girls who read this book will probably be in the first part of the cycle, when they need the information given them here to understand how their bodies are constructed, and the encouragement to investigate and appreciate how really marvelously equipped they are to function as one half of the male-female relationship.

The culmination of physical development in a girl usually comes at about the time she reaches sixteen. Girls who have arrived at that age and still haven't reached physical maturity should remember the wide variation that exists in the human female, as well as the male. Some girls reach full development as far as growth and height are concerned by the time they're ten or eleven years old. Others don't achieve it until they're twenty-one or older. And even when growth and height are complete, there is still further development in the breasts and the growth of pubic hair; the girl's figure may, in fact, keep on filling out for some time until it has reached the proportions she will have as a woman.

As you can see, adolescence can be a joyous and happy time, but it's also unquestionably a time of change and adjustment. For some that may mean anxiety and fear, but the girl who has a good knowledge of her body will find it much easier to enjoy the process of growing up that every girl must go through.

CHAPTER 3
Early Sexual Experiences

Boys and girls are usually curious when they're growing up about what the sex organs of the opposite sex look like. By the time they're five years old, about six out of ten girls have seen a boy's penis. Often their first sight of it is of a younger brother's while he's being bathed or diapered as his sister watches. It's a fact, however, that one out of ten girls who have reached the age of thirteen still hasn't seen the penis of a living male. Even if she has a baby brother, her parents may keep the girl carefully protected from viewing it. That, of course, only whets the girl's interest in seeing something forbidden. At the worst, it may make her fearful and ashamed to look at a penis, a sure source of trouble later on.

Whatever the intentions of parents may be, hiding the penis won't have the good result they intend. Not only can it result in psychological damage, but it's futile in any case, because a girl who reads magazines or illustrated art books or takes art classes in school soon enough sees the penis reproduced in works of painting and sculpture. The great masters have reproduced it endlessly through the ages, just as they have depicted the entire male body in all its splendor. Museums are filled with their testimonials to the beauty of the human form, both male and female. If a young girl has been given the idea that the penis (and the nude male body) is ugly or repulsive, she will have a great deal to overcome when she arrives at the point of having sexual relationships with men.

The girl who sees her little brother's or some other boy's penis in the casual pattern of everyday living learns to accept this male organ as a fact of life. If it's hidden from her, she keeps wondering about it, and the secrecy may contribute to later troubles in her sex life.

Before girls become adolescent, about half of them have seen their father's penis or that of an older male relative. That means little more to them than seeing a baby's or a small boy's penis. These are simply things males have, and their curiosity about males is at least partially satisfied. Seeing the male sexual organ and having sexual contact with adult males are two different things, however, and I'll discuss that problem later on in this chapter.

It's always been a natural part of a child's development to look at and explore the bodies of other young children, to examine the similarities and differences, and to get some sexual pleasure from doing it. Parents often forbid this harmless sexual activity. It's naughty, they say, but then they're shocked and surprised when children try even harder to do this naughty thing their parents are forbidding. They find extra excitement in doing it *because* it's forbidden. So children go right on playing the childhood games they've always played— mama and papa, doctor and nurse—the same games the parents played too, but which some of them seem to have forgotten. Young children use these games as a way to look at and explore each other's bodies.

Once children learn that these activities are "naughty"—and sometimes they learn it from other children—they rarely tell their parents they're doing it. Consequently, when many parents accidentally discover that their children are having sex play, they are very upset and blow up the incident out of all proportion to its real significance. When such a scene takes place, the generation gap begins to open up, and unless things change, it won't be long before parents find themselves unable to talk openly to their children about sex. For their part, the children continue to carry on their sex lives and normal sexual development secretly.

The fact is that there's nothing in the least unusual or "dangerous" about this early sex play. Half the time it consists of nothing more than looking at the organs of the opposite sex. A girl may touch the boy's penis, and the boy will touch her vulva. It's a process of exploring with the hands rather than with the eyes. Occasionally very young boys and girls may try having intercourse with each other. In most cases, no actual penetration by the penis occurs. It's more a matter of the boy getting on top of the girl and going through the motions. Rarely at this age do they understand what actually happens in intercourse. A few (but very few) try to insert something into the girl's vagina—a finger or a stick—and even fewer have the idea of trying to put their mouths on another's sex organ.

For nearly all girls, such early play is done without any sexual arousal on their part. Perhaps only one out of ten gets a feeling she can identify later as an arousal. For the few girls who *are* aroused, however, the experience can lead to orgasm (see Chapter 6), one as full and complete and satisfying as those they will have when they're older. Even baby girls, less than a year old, are quite capable of having these orgasms, and sometimes they do.

In general, girls tend to have more sex play at younger ages, from four to nine years of age, than they do at older ages, from ten to thirteen. For half the girls who experience early sex play, it is something that happens only once, or two or three times at the most. For the others, it will happen oftener and the experiences may be spread out over the entire pre-adolescent period.

Girls also sometimes have sex play with other girls. This happens about as often as sex play with boys. It's also usually exploration and curiosity, rather than deliberate attempts at sexual arousal. With about a third of children, such play is concerned only with looking, while the other two thirds go so far as to touch. In two out of ten cases, it will involve inserting fingers or other objects into the vagina—and incidentally, this happens much more frequently between girls than between boys and girls. Rarely, as in sex play with boys, do these experiences between girls involve what we call "oral-genital"—that is, the mouth on the sex organ.

By and large, boys are more inclined to have sex play before adolescence than girls are. Not infrequently one girl may be involved in sex play with two or more boys at the same time, but less frequently is a single boy involved with two or more girls simultaneously. Boys are also more likely to start sex play with girls than the other way around.

Sex play with boys (or, for that matter, with girls) can be exciting, pleasurable, and even worthwhile in the sense that it will help later sexual adjustment. But there are three difficulties that make it complicated. One is the possibility of being found out by parents or other adults, and so having the experience exaggerated beyond its simple significance. A child is likely to be punished, or made to feel unworthy or wicked in some other way, because most adults are convinced such behavior is wrong and dangerous.

The second difficulty is somewhat like the first. Other children involved in sex play often reflect adult attitudes about sex, even though they may be taking part in the play themselves. If they know someone else has been caught doing it, they may ridicule the girl who has been found out, or her playmates may shut her out of their circle.

The third problem is the feeling of guilt that some girls develop whether they are caught or not. The realization that such play must be kept secret and that it's disapproved leads to feelings of being naughty and of being not worthwhile.

Girls reading this book have probably lived through that part of their lives, and so whatever they did one way or the other is in the past. But those who did have sex play as children may be able to see now that there were positive and worthwhile aspects about it, no matter what negative things may have bothered them. They may be able, now, to put those "bad" things in a better perspective.

As the first chapter noted, boys are much more specific in their sexual interests than girls are. It isn't surprising, then, that older men get interested in young girls and hope for some sort of sexual response from them. At least a quarter of the girls who reach adolescence have been approached by older men, or perhaps have even had direct sexual contact with them. By the time they're seventeen, nearly all girls have had such approaches made to them in one way or another.

These approaches are often harmless, like the appreciative whistles from strangers on the street or from passing truck drivers. They range from such whistles to what may be a half-joking sexual advance from a girl friend's father, who puts his arm around her from behind and presses on her breasts, or strokes her buttocks affectionately, or likes to put his arms around her. Again, it may be the loving uncle who enjoys patting his niece's thigh or some other part of her anatomy. Even more frequently, perhaps, it may be a direct sexual advance from a young father who is taking the baby-sitter home. Approaches can be merely verbal, or they can go as far as exposing the penis or touching a girl's sex organ or, if a man gets the response he hopes for, actual intercourse.

Girls are often embarrassed and bewildered about how to handle these situations. They may feel threatened by them and uncomfortable. These approaches are usually uninvited and unexpected, but sometimes girls, whether they realize it or not, encourage a man to make the advance.

Let's talk first about the ones that are uninvited. When she's being approached by an older man and hasn't invited it, one of the things a girl can do is to let him know flatly and at once that she isn't interested. No need to be hysterical about it—just firm. If a girl is confused and taken aback by the advance, she may well be hesitant and silent, not knowing what to say or do, utterly embarrassed by the whole thing and unable to handle the situation. Unfortunately, a man is likely to take her silence for consent, even though she is far from consenting. A complicating factor is that such a young girl feels herself in the presence of a more powerful person, an authority figure like her parents, and believes she can't deal with him as she would a boy of her own age.

But she ought to remember that it's a situation where she has every right to let her feelings be known;

and afterward, aware of what has happened, she will be much more careful not to let herself be put in such a position again. Sometimes, though, it can't be anticipated, as in the case of the girl friend's father, or the father of the baby she's been sitting with. In these situations, a good idea is to think of it as no different from being out with a boy you don't like well enough to pet with. The tentative advances he makes are about the same thing, and it's entirely proper not to be awed by his greater age and authority.

There are many situations, however, in which a girl consciously or unconsciously invites approaches from older men. Sometimes the sheer pleasure of knowing that an older man is attracted to her or has singled her out to pay attention to makes her act in a flirtatious or seductive manner. Then things may get out of hand because the man becomes more aggressive than the girl likes or knows how to handle.

Sometimes men (mostly strangers) expose their penises to a young girl because of psychological problems that drive them to it. They may do this in the mistaken hope a young girl will become interested. More often, however, they do it to provoke a reaction of shock, revulsion, or surprise. Men who do this are almost never dangerous, and the best possible way to deal with them is to show complete indifference and keep cool. Confronted with such a situation, the girl may think that it's the exhibited penis that's ugly and repulsive. In reality, it's the circumstances surrounding the incident that are repellent, not the penis itself.

Another not uncommon experience occurs when a girl goes alone to the movies and a man sitting beside her slips a hand under her thigh or otherwise makes some kind of sexual advance. The remedy is a simple one. Get up and move to another seat. If he persists, complain to the manager.

Society may frown on sex play between children, but we have to remember that society disapproves of a great many sexual acts that take place, and there are two sides to the story. Granted, there are sometimes good reasons for the disapproval, but on the other hand, there is also a large amount of overreaction to sex on society's part. If a girl has had sex play with girls and boys of her own age, these experiences may have been or will be of value to her, whether they turned out well or badly. If badly, she may have learned as she would from any other unhappy and upsetting experience. Otherwise, she will have learned something positive—about the way her own body works and what its reactions can be, and something about other people, too. Pleasure has been given and received. All these things have their value for the future.

CHAPTER 4
Dating

Dating should be an easy, pleasant matter—a learning process paving the way to adult relationships, both sexual and nonsexual. Often it is, but as every teenager knows, there are few areas of boy-girl relationships where more problems arise. Parents know it too, and teachers know it, but most of all, often painfully and with some heartache, girls and boys know it.

Too often adults smile and dismiss this adolescent struggle as part of the business of growing up, which of course it is, but that doesn't mean there isn't anything to be done about it. It's natural to be disturbed by dating problems, but better understanding can improve any kind of human relationship, and dating is no exception.

One of the first things to understand is the marked difference in the way girls and boys grow up at this stage of their lives, which accounts for a good part of the trouble. The basic difficulty is that, on the whole, girls grow up faster than boys. Their height starts increasing rapidly a year or more before the boys begin to shoot up, and for thirteen- and fourteen-year-olds, this difference creates a potentially embarrassing situation. A girl finds that she's suddenly begun to look over the head of the boy she has liked and played with since they were children, and it may be two or three years before they are back on even terms. Meanwhile, social customs being what they are, girls may not want to go out with boys who are shorter; and quite naturally, many boys, who are just beginning to date about this time, find such discrimination hard to understand. Consequently, younger girls who haven't begun to grow that much may find themselves dating boys a little older than they are. But other girls are late starters or naturally shorter, so there may be some evening up of opportunities.

Girls also mature earlier than boys. The pubic hair around the girl's sex organ usually grows before the male's, and her breasts enlarge before the corresponding breast knots on the boy begin to swell. On the average, she menstruates about a year before the boy is able to ejaculate. There's a reverse difference here, however. The boy has sperm in his semen from the first, while it's probably true, although not absolutely proven, that a girl does not produce egg cells that are capable of fertilization at the time of her first menstruation. It may take her several months or even years before that process, called "ovulation," begins. We know, however, that this isn't true of all girls.

As I've pointed out earlier, an important difference at this stage is the fact that most boys suddenly become intensely interested in sex, while most girls do not. Girls *are* interested in boys in a way they haven't been before, but they think of their new relationship in terms of dating and having a good time, whereas the boy is sexually excited and feels an urge, perhaps unconsciously, toward ejaculation. Girls seldom know how boys are feeling at this particular time, and most of them are quite surprised if they find out they've excited a boy sexually by flirting or petting. As far as the girl is concerned, it's only another kind of friendship.

But in spite of these or any other difficulties, dating is something both sexes want very much to do. This urge raises the question that bothers so many girls, and boys, too: "How do I get a date?" So many are eager to start, but don't know quite how to begin.

A girl might think about the problem in familiar terms. It's like going to buy a dress. If a girl wants new clothes, she has to go to a store that sells dresses—and it's the same thing with boys. Girls sometimes say they want to go "where the boys are," and when they do, they're shopping, whether they think of it that way or not.

The easiest place to look, of course, is in school, where girls are in daily contact with boys their own age. Most dating begins right there. Students in girls' schools have a little more difficult time, but even there, school authorities frequently arrange parties and other events to bring boys and girls together. There are other places, too. Young people's groups in community clubs or churches are good places to meet boys. Sometimes parents take their daughters on summer vacations where they have opportunities, and summer jobs of all kinds, at resorts or in the city, provide further chances. Still another approach is to choose girl friends who are already dating. That often leads to meeting friends of their friends.

Meeting boys is sometimes easy, sometimes difficult, but in either case, it's only the beginning. Many girls try all the approaches I've mentioned, and still they don't have dates. Why? Most commonly it's because of a girl's attitude toward herself. I tell such girls: "It's difficult for other people, including boys, to like you unless you like yourself."

At first they may not understand what I mean, because it's common belief that people grow to like themselves as other people demonstrate a liking for them. It's the other way around, however. Self-approval is a highly important element in living happily, and it comes from the individual's view of himself or herself.

What does it really mean to "like yourself"? For one thing, it means a girl isn't obsessed with her physical imperfections. She isn't absorbed in the knowledge that her teeth are slightly crooked, or that she has a lot of freckles, or her hair isn't the color she wishes it were, or her figure isn't as good as her friend's. Physical qualities are far from being the whole of beauty. Some of the most beautiful girls I've known would never be able to get into a beauty contest. And conversely, some beauty-contest winners have been the worst possible candidates for establishing a good relationship with a boy. Girls who think that boys like only the prettiest girls are looking at the wrong boys.

Those who are hung up on how beautiful a girl is aren't good candidates for dating.

Many aspects of a girl's relationship with herself can get in the way of successful dating. There are girls who have personality problems of different kinds, such as those who are in such extreme rebellion against their parents that this situation becomes very nearly the most important thing in their lives. Others are in constant conflict with their brothers and sisters, and that absorbs their emotions. Others have strong guilt feelings over things they may have done and can't lift their eyes above the high wall these feelings have erected between them and the world. Then there are the lonely girls, usually painfully shy. All these girls have the poorest prospects for getting dates.

The obstacle raised by such personality difficulties is that a girl becomes so concerned with herself and her problems that she's unable to see a boy as an individual in his own right, a human being with his own feelings and desires. She sees him and everything else only in relation to herself. That's what I mean when I tell girls they have to like themselves before other people will like them. It doesn't mean being egotistical. It means they must believe they're as good as anyone else.

You may be muttering by this time, "That's a lot of preaching. How do I start liking myself?" I have to admit there's no easy answer to this question, and I wouldn't pretend there was. But I *am* certain that any girl can make a start simply by recognizing that she's going to be much happier if she understands something has to be done and begins to make an inventory of her own personality to see where she needs to change.

Oddly enough, some girls have difficulty recognizing the most self-evident thing about themselves. Pretty girls often deny they're pretty, and are even embarrassed when someone tells them they are. They need to accept the fact that they're attractive and make the most of their natural charm. It will take them far in all kinds of relationships. On the other hand, there are even more girls who are convinced they're *not* attractive, but it usually turns out that they realize they're not as physically good-looking as some other girl they're comparing themselves with. They put themselves down on the basis of something entirely superficial. There are plenty of girls who aren't pretty, or even reasonably good-looking, who are sought after because they're such good and interesting companions, or because their personalities are sparkling, or for other reasons that have nothing to do with conventional beauty.

A girl needs to assess herself honestly, decide what her best points are, and work on developing them. At the same time, she should try to see herself in relation to other people—girls as well as boys. If she's shy, she can work on that; it can be overcome. If she can't express herself well, that isn't hard to cure either if she works on it. The important thing is to focus on your best qualities, learn to think well of yourself because you have them, and relate yourself to other people. If you have nonphysical bad qualities that you recognize—a too quick temper, for example—you can work on them too. People change, and they can change themselves. It happens every day. It just takes honesty and a little work.

A feeling of rejection is often at the root of many of these difficulties. If your father or your mother or someone else rejects you, or you feel that they're doing so, that may or may not be true, but in any case, it doesn't mean you deserve to be rejected or that other people feel the same way. It may well be just the opposite. Boys won't reject a girl if she won't do *everything* they want her to. It's far better to be independent, to be your own self.

That means realizing, too, that boys and marriage, or some other relationship, aren't the only things in life for girls anymore. You need to think about what you're going to do with your life in its nonsexual aspects, which means most of it. There is a firm relationship, however. If you're able to relate well to boys in dating, which includes having the proper image of yourself, it will help you to relate to the men you will associate with later on, in your business or profession or in your intimate relations with them, whether that means marriage or living with someone. You can only learn to have good relationships with the opposite sex by doing what you have to do in learning anything

59

else—practice. How to relate to another person—and in general how to be a responsive person—takes a lot of practice and much self-knowledge.

But let's assume now that you don't have any personality problems of consequence and that you're able to meet boys. The next most common problem—and one that often brings a girl into conflict with her parents—is when to start dating. Parents and girls alike have asked me anxiously about the proper time to begin. The only answer seems too simple to be true, but it is. The right time is when a girl *feels* that it's the right time. Dating is, first of all, a matter of two people pairing off to get to know each other better, but in the background is the fact that one is male, the other female, and this difference may possibly lead to some kind of physical contact and some kind of emotional relationship based on feelings that are more than simple friendship.

By "the right time," then, I mean the time when a girl thinks she is ready to develop a boy-girl relationship that has potentialities. For the boy, these potentialities are pretty specifically sexual—kissing, petting, even intercourse. For the girl, it means the possibility of being liked and accepted—singled out as a special person. To a girl, moreover, a date has the special meaning of having a boy interested enough in her to take her places. That gives her a sense of her own importance, a sense of status.

The beginning of dating, as I've said, may be the beginning of a conflict with parents. That conflict arises because, at the time when a girl feels she's ready to date, the chances are that her parents think it's too early. Then she faces the problem of either disobeying her parents or not dating until they permit it.

It helps, I think, for everyone to realize first that what they're going through is an inevitable part of growing up, and it's hard on both parents and chilren. If they think about the conflict with their parents hard enough, it should be clear to the children that the real issue is responsibility. Parents want to feel that their girls and boys are going to behave responsibly when they're away from home in a new situation. If a girl shows that she's responsible in smaller things, perhaps there will be less objection to having her begin dating.

If it's impossible to discuss the whole thing sensibly with parents, or if they're simply adamant about it, a good many girls will date anyway—and under the worst circumstances, because they'll have to sneak around and lie about it instead of enjoying this new experience easily and naturally. It may be the first time a girl really confronts the whole question of honesty with parents about something fundamental. I hope a girl in this situation will examine her own set of values carefully and try to decide whether it's more important to her to be honest with her parents or to do what the other girls are doing. Unfortunately, both courses have their drawbacks, and she'll have to face the drawbacks honestly too.

It comes down to a question of obeying parents and

giving up temporarily some of the things you want to do—things the other girls are doing—or going ahead and subsequently suffering guilt feelings, with the fear of getting caught in the back of your mind. A girl may be further ahead in the end sometimes by asserting her independence and refusing to go along with the others simply because "everybody's doing it." In the situation I've been talking about, that kind of independence won't permit you to start dating, but it may earn you some respect and admiration from your contemporaries.

Girls who are having problems with their parents over dating or over boyfriends are in need of some older person they can talk to—not someone who's going to moralize or judge them, or give them advice, but someone who'll just listen and understand. It's a lucky girl who has parents who can do this much for her. Sometimes a teacher can help, or a guidance counselor, or a loved relative. I'm not suggesting that the older person, whoever it is, is wiser or "knows better." I'm only saying that such a person, by listening sympathetically, helps a girl to clarify the problem in her own mind. It's another way of helping her feel better about herself.

But let's assume you don't have any of these problems, and that you're already happily dating. Either boys are calling you for dates, or sometimes you're calling one of them. That last wouldn't have been considered a good thing to do even ten years ago, and before then, it was considered something no girl in her right mind would think of. Today, however, it's perfectly proper and natural for a girl to ask a boy for a date. It needn't be aggressive, just a sharing of mutual interests. There's something you want to do or see, and you know a boy you'd like to date would be likely to want the same thing. Easy enough to talk to him about it, and say, "Let's go there together," or, "I heard this new disco is really great, why don't we go and try it?"

One way or the other, then, you're dating. The next big question is whether or not to go steady—another phrase that sounds old-fashioned today, but again there's no substitute for saying, "Seeing someone else regularly and not going out with someone else." There are often conflicting ideas about this too. In fact, if there's one subject in a girl's sexual and social development where advice is not lacking, this is it.

There's something to be said on both sides, of course. A girl who goes steady has a welcome sense of security—that is, wherever she wants to go, she always has a date and no lonely evenings. Besides, there's the undeniable fact that going steady permits a deeper emotional relationship to develop between two people than does "playing the field."

But there's also something to be said against it. If a girl dates a good many boys, she'll have a better opportunity of finding out what kind of male she wants to live with eventually, if she does want to do so—which personality traits in a boy attract her and which ones make her unhappy. She may find out that moody, irritable boys don't suit her easygoing, essentially optimistic way of living. Or that boys with sharp tempers frighten her. Or that sloppy boys get on her nerves if her inclination is toward neatness—or, for that matter, the other way around. She'll be able to see clearly the difference between an uncaring person and one who is warm and loving. These experiences help a girl to make up her mind later about what kind of person she chooses to share her life with, no matter what the relationship, and it may save her from bad and risky situations in the future.

All this isn't to say that girls necessarily wind up having relationships with the kind of men who are best for them. Some girls, in fact, have a reverse talent. But more often than not, early experiences do affect the eventual choice of deep relationships.

Another advantage of not going steady is that a girl finds herself in a far greater variety of social situations, meeting new parents, making more new friends, and this is good experience in learning how to construct a satisfactory social life, besides being satisfying in itself.

There's one very real danger in going steady, and I'm sure every girl who reads this has heard it said, but it bears repeating. In our society, many of those who begin going steady early end up by marrying either while they are still in high school or just after graduation. Ten years or so later, both women and men in these marriages often wake up to the realization that there are a lot of other people in the world and a great many other experiences, both sexual and otherwise, that they've missed by settling so early for one person. A good part of the precious freedom which is the property of the young is gone, and it won't come back. These young couples, still in their early twenties and usually with one or more children, feel themselves trapped, perhaps more often than not, and a good many get themselves untrapped, as the divorce statistics show. You can make a new start with a divorce, but that action itself is usually not an easy matter psychologically, even in the best circumstances, and starting over at a later stage isn't so easy.

Today the dating pattern that seems to be most common is neither going steady nor playing the field to the limit, but rather periods of close, steady friendship with one person, followed by dating several boys.

On the date itself, the chief questions that arise are those of behavior. Here the differences between the sexes that I've mentioned become most important. Girls are more concerned about their reputations than boys are, even in the new liberated era, and how far they go in petting, for example, is often determined more by what they think the boy is going to tell other boys than by anything else.

When a boy starts to kiss a girl, her reaction may not be, "Isn't this fun? What have I been waiting for?" but, "I wonder what he'll think about me," and, "Will he tell the other boys and what will *they* think?" It's too bad that our social system produces this kind of reaction, even though it doesn't always happen by any means. But as long as we keep on playing the ridiculous game of "good girl" and "bad girl," the best thing a girl can do is to have confidence in herself and in the way she sees herself relating to the world around her. If she does that, she may not get involved in sexual situations before she's emotionally ready for them.

It makes more sense, I believe, for a girl to decide rationally how far she wants to go in a particular situation with a particular boy than to be constantly concerned about her reputation. It's extremely difficult to be rational, I know, when a girl is emotionally involved in a situation, and there's no easy solution. A girl simply has to think about it, or not think about it, but at least she should understand that she has a clear choice.

Certainly there ought to be a better reason than concern over what other people think to guide a girl in how far she should go. Some girls go farther than they want to because they're afraid their date will tell other boys that they're "frigid" or "prudish."

Earlier, I talked about what a handicap it was for a girl who wanted to date to be involved in her own problems; concentrating on "reputation" can be in the same category. It's important for a girl to allow herself the *freedom* to be interested in what interests her date, and that can be done only if she's free of her own hang-ups. There's a familiar gag line that goes, "Let's talk about *you* for a while. What do you think of me?" There are far too many girls who behave just like that. It's the sort of thing a girl should never do on a date. She should carefully avoid such subjects as the state of her health, the problems she has with her hair, her experiences with other boys, and—well, any girl can add to that list. Boys could make it even longer.

It's a problem of communicating, of the ability to express feelings whether positive or negative, and the ability to respond to the feelings others express. But communicating means more than just talking. For example, a girl can *talk* about a coming school dance, but she *communicates* her feelings about going to it. Communicating feelings is more dangerous, because a girl makes herself more vulnerable, more open. Yet a good relationship with another person, boy or girl, involves this very openness and this very danger. The kind of communication I'm talking about has to be honest and sincere, without worry about its effect on the other person. In short, a girl should be herself— natural, open, not exclusively concerned with making an impression on others.

In that respect, girls can help boys. Boys need to understand the role they ought to play in boy-girl relationships. There are all kinds of small social gestures that go with relationships in our society, and these days people are likely to forget them. Boys have seen too many antihero, tough-guy movies, for example. And it isn't necessarily a matter of perpetuating old conventions between the sexes. It's a courtesy to another human being, which many girls and women still appreciate, when a boy helps a girl on with her coat (or vice versa), or opens a car door, or carries her books if they're obviously a heavy load. Nor is it a question of right or wrong. A girl who subtly encourages a boy to remember these little things is emphasizing in another way the boy-girl relationship, and that's what dating is all about. By helping a date observe these ancient customs, a girl helps to develop the male-female bond between them she wants to establish.

Another complication in dating—and it can be a serious one—is the problem of age differences. Girls often want to know how much older a boy can be and still be an acceptable date. Obviously, there's no simple answer. A boy's actual age, for example, may be far different from his emotional age. Then, too, a girl often finds it gratifying to have the attention of an older boy, or even a man, because it makes her feel more special under such circumstances.

Consider, for instance, a thirteen-year-old girl who is dating a junior or senior in high school. This can be a worthwhile relationship if it's based on common interests and mutual attraction. However, it will help a girl and perhaps save her from trouble if she asks herself what other reasons the older boy might have for dating her. Is he emotionally mature? Is he thinking of her only as a possible sexual conquest because she's exceptionally attractive, even though she's so much younger? If the answer to any of these questions is yes, a girl may want to reconsider dating him, in spite of being excited about the flattering attention she's getting.

As the age difference increases, the problems increase. Here's the same girl, but this time she's dating a twenty-one-year-old boy, just back home from college on vacation perhaps, or out of school and working. Again, it's possible for two such people to have a good and meaningful relationship, but now the odds are more heavily against it. The same questions ought to be asked, particularly the one about his emotional maturity.

There's an even longer step this hypothetical girl can take, one that would apply even more to girls who are older. She may be dating, secretly, the thirty-five-year-old father of the child for whom she baby-sits. It's possible that even this relationship could be a positive one, but the odds are so heavily against its turning out to be anything but disastrous that nothing can really be expected from it except unhappiness. True, it may be exciting and fun to be noticed by such a man. But to generalize about it, the greater the age difference, the greater the chance that the older man has some psychological problem. Almost invariably a girl's interests will be different, and the relationship is virtually certain to end badly.

Dating married men of any age, and particularly falling in love with one, is an invitation to trouble and heartbreak. A girl must realize that, no matter what he may tell her or how convincingly he says it, the odds are at least a thousand to one that he won't divorce his wife and marry her. Neither his unhappiness at home nor his love for the girl are likely to be decisive factors when the crunch comes, as it inevitably will. To go through the sheer agony of divorce, often with the wife fighting it, is too much for a man to contemplate. This is something his teenage girl friend will not understand.

A girl who finds herself in this situation should not deceive herself about the outcome or about the man involved. If she's willing to put up with empty weekends, surreptitious meetings, and be content with having only part of a man, then she's entitled to whatever short-range satisfaction she can get. I know that each individual situation is special and different. The girl who's dating a married man firmly believes that, in her case, the odds are much more in her favor than they really are. But if she's able to stop deceiving herself long enough to examine her situation honestly, she may discover that things are different from what she thought. Often, if she's able to talk openly and freely to someone who's not directly involved with her life, it will help her see the situation more clearly.

Of all the questions a counselor hears from very young girls, I suppose the most frequent is the plaintive query: "How do I know I'm in love?"

First, love is not sex. They are separate things, although they may occur together. A girl loves her parents or her dog or her best friend, without the involvement of sex. On the other hand, it's possible to have sex with someone without loving that person. Many times love and sexual feelings are part of the same response, and when that combination occurs, it can be one of the most profound and meaningful experiences human beings are capable of having. Being "in love" isn't something distinct and separate from being "not in love." If we put it on a scale, the range would be from zero to a hundred. At one end somewhere would be the feelings a girl has for a boy she likes and sometimes dates. As she knows him better and they date more often, her feelings move upward on the scale until the time comes when she feels warm and excited to be with him, wants to be with him as much as possible, and would rather be with him than with anyone else. At that point a girl could say with some confidence, "I'm in love." But that doesn't mean she's reached the opposite end of the scale. There's a distance to go, perhaps, and since love is not exactly a fixed and stable emotion, she may go up and down the scale for a time. Affection may be followed by sexual feelings and a depth of emotion far from what it was at the beginning. If it was "puppy love," it will never have gone so far. That comes quickly and goes quickly, no matter how painful it may seem at the time.

At the far end of the scale is love, real love, solid and unmistakable. It's based on trust, understanding, consideration, and open communication, and it's very much worth having.

I've been talking in these pages about the sexual aspects of a girl's life, because that's what the book is about, but I hope no girl reading it will underestimate the importance of love or fail to see that sex is only one of the many faces of love. It's possible to have sex without love, and love without sex, but it's the blending of the two that produces one of the most satisfying and rewarding of human experiences. A girl's sexual feelings for a boy may not lead to intercourse, until the time she believes it's appropriate, but they become important only as they reinforce her total feeling of commitment, trust, and understanding—in a word, love.

CHAPTER 5
Petting

Again I have to use a word that may seem old-fashioned to you since we don't have a good modern equivalent for "petting." Everybody still knows what it means, however, but the meaning is different in various parts of the country and from one age group to another. Some people think of it as tongue-kissing (also once called "soul-kissing" and the "French kiss"). Others believe some touching of the sex organ has to take place before it can be called "petting." My definition is that any physical contact of a sexual nature is petting. "Making out" was a more recent substitute, and "getting it off" is current, although that more generally means intercourse, but we can be sure that other words and phrases will come along in time to describe this most common of sexual exchanges.

To describe it further, let me say that I believe petting, by any name, is a way of communicating sexual feelings to another person. But unless it's mutual, there can't be anything very meaningful about it. Consequently, it's probably best to discourage petting if a girl feels she can't accept the feeling a boy is trying to communicate to her. She should understand, too, that a boy may be so aroused himself that he forgets about her response and doesn't care whether she's responding or not. That's the time to cut it off, but gently, diplomatically.

Petting involves (or should involve) some degree of affection and emotional feeling, as well as an interest in and appreciation of the other person, but it's also a prelude to intercourse. Almost all intercourse is preceded by it—and then it is called "foreplay." That implication is always there in petting, and a girl should be aware of it and govern herself accordingly.

One of the advantages of petting as a learning process is that it has a progression, from one step to another, and progress can be stopped at any point. At its simplest it consists of hugging someone warmly—a universal gesture of affection that everyone needs, whether the intent is sexual or not. This is probably the most common demonstration of affection in our society. If petting follows, however, the next step is kissing. A girl who has never kissed a boy finds these first kisses a little awkward and probably not very exciting.

When she's old enough and ready to be aroused, excitement will make her lips go soft and open, so that the next step inevitably occurs—tongue-kissing. From there petting proceeds, usually, to the boy's putting a hand on a girl's breast outside her clothing, then inside, and then perhaps to touching his mouth to the breast. It's only a short step from there to putting the hands on the sex organ—the boy's or the girl's—

outside the clothing, and then inside. Sometimes a boy puts his mouth on the vulva of a girl, she puts her mouth on his penis, or they may do this at the same time. But that's most likely to occur just before intercourse, if this is to be the end result of the petting, although it can also happen by itself.

Petting is such a common, delightful experience that it hardly needs to be justified, but maybe it should be said, once again, that it's a pleasurable experience that not only creates exciting body sensations but may lead to orgasm. It's a wonderful feeling, enjoyed by people everywhere in the world. Another advantage is that there's no possibility of pregnancy, except in those extremely rare cases where the boy ejaculates at the opening of the vagina and the sperm work their way through the entire length of the vagina and up into the uterus. Still another advantage is that the possibility of communicating venereal disease is equally remote, although if there is mouth-genital contact, infection is possible.

Petting is also extremely useful as a learning experience for later relationships, perhaps one that's better than intercourse itself. A boy ought to know how to stimulate a girl properly, and she ought to know what it's like to be stimulated. This stimulation is learned through the techniques of petting, and because petting embraces a whole variety of contacts, from kissing to mouth-genital contact, it can be learned in gradual steps. Every new step can be assimilated and become a part of a girl's emotional knowledge, of herself and of boys. It's been argued in the past that petting can be harmful because it may fix a girl at this level so that she won't enjoy intercourse later, but there's no truth in this, unless there are psychological problems that keep a girl from enjoying intercourse. These problems aren't caused by the petting experience.

As I've noted, a girl may not particularly like petting when she first begins and will naturally go slowly. In the ordinary course of events, however, she learns to like it as she progresses from one step to another. But she must remember that the boy will want to go much faster than she does, and she'll have to make him slow down so that she can keep up. This isn't true in every case, of course; it depends a lot on the girl's background and nature. But if she wants to go slowly, she should explain to the boy gently how she feels, and if he cares enough about her as a person, he'll respect her feelings.

Girls discover quickly that boys want to pet them and will go as far as they're permitted. Some girls use this fact, unconsciously or consciously, as a kind of lever for bargaining with a boy. If he's been particularly attentive or has taken her to an especially nice place, she may allow him to go further than she would permit him to otherwise. But if she feels that she's been shortchanged on the date, she may refuse him anything more than a good-night kiss, if that. "What does he expect for a lousy hamburger and a cup of coffee?" is the familiar cry. That's exactly the wrong approach to petting. It isn't an exchange of favors—

"I'll give you something in proportion to what you do for me." It's an exchange of mutual feelings in which nothing else ought to be involved.

If a girl happens to be feeling hostile or irritated about something, she may sometimes deliberately let the boy get aroused in a petting situation and then refuse to continue, as a means of punishing him. It isn't hard to understand that using sex this way, as a weapon, is not only obviously unfair but closes off the kind of open communication that makes a relationship desirable.

Because it's difficult for a young and inexperienced girl to understand how much more sexually oriented boys are than she is, she may often, without having any understanding of what she's doing, say or do provocative things that will be constantly frustrating to a boy, particularly if petting doesn't follow. Sometimes it's only a matter of vocabulary, of double meanings not intended. For example, a girl may say at the end of a date, "My parents are in bed. Come on in and we'll have a good time."

By that she may mean nothing more than listening to some music and having something to eat without parents being around. Most likely, however, a boy will translate her casual remark as, "The coast is clear and we can pet." Then he finds out that what he thinks is an open invitation is something else, and the girl is shocked by his advances and resists them. The result: he's left irritated and frustrated because he's picked up the wrong cue.

Again, after a long kiss during petting, a girl might say, "Gee, I'm hot!" The boy translates this as, "I'm all aroused and ready to go," and takes the next step, or tries to. But the girl may have meant simply that she was warm and beginning to perspire; it won't occur to her that anyone would misinterpret her literal way of expressing herself. It helps if girls keep in mind how much more sexually oriented boys are, and that remarks they make will usually be interpreted in that way.

Boys have a short, descriptive word for girls who deliberately get them worked up and then back off, leaving them frustrated. The word is "cockteaser." You may think it's an ugly word, but it accurately describes a practice that is clearly unfair and tells us something about the personality of the girl who does it. Such behavior may be unconscious with some girls. They don't understand what they're doing, or what effect it's having, because of their inexperience or ignorance, and they're surprised and indignant when a boy responds aggressively to being treated that way. If matters are explained to such a girl and she understands what's happened, she'll be much better able to decide what she wants to do about petting.

Another kind of girl, however, is a different proposition. She knows perfectly well what she's doing and does it out of malice, spite, or resentment. She's an actress, playing the lead role in a drama of hostility because, for deep-seated and complicated reasons, she doesn't like males in general and chooses this way to get even with them. A few tease for a different reason. Other girls have convinced them that it's the smart thing to do and may even show them how to do it. Then there are those who want to dominate males, and tease because it's a way of controlling boys and showing aggression.

Girls who have an orgasm when they're petting are doing themselves a favor, because if they have orgasms when they're young, they will have an easier time, generally speaking, in making good sexual adjustments in their adult relationships. Of all the ways to have an orgasm, petting to that point is probably the most helpful. If a girl becomes aroused sexually in petting, however, and then doesn't have an orgasm, she often feels frustrated and unsatisfied. If it occurs over and over again, it builds up habit patterns difficult to break in later life.

Sometimes, too, petting without orgasm leaves her with pains in her groin that can be very uncomfortable. About half the girls who are aroused during petting have that experience, and about a third of them masturbate afterward to relieve tension. Either continuing to pet until orgasm occurs or masturbating later are certainly better methods than to live with this frustration and uneasiness.

Girls (and parents too) ought not to overemphasize petting. It's surprising but true that even in the present climate of freedom there are still a large number of girls who haven't petted at all by the time they finish high school, and a majority haven't started to pet by the time they're thirteen or fourteen. Most of them, however, do begin petting sometime in their early teens, and there are comparatively few who enter adult life without ever having done it. Petting to orgasm has become much more common in the past decade, and it will probably continue to increase. For girls who aren't ready yet for intercourse, it solves the problem of how to learn to respond sexually to boys, and that's an important thing to learn. Petting and self-masturbation are probably the most acceptable kinds of sexual behavior among adolescent girls.

While there may be only a little more actual sexual behavior in this generation than in the previous one, it's true that teenagers today do drink more alcohol, and as everyone knows, their use of drugs has become a national problem.

Boys sometimes think alcohol is the best way to stimulate a girl to sex. They know that *they* feel more uninhibited and amorous when they've been drinking, and they think a girl feels the same way. Since they imagine themselves more alert and sensitive to every kind of stimulation when they drink, they're convinced that, with the aid of alcohol, any boy and girl can drink themselves into sex.

In a way, that's true. There's no doubt that alcohol removes some inhibitions. But it *is* a depressant rather than a stimulant, and only a small amount (a drink or two) is necessary to depress the higher nervous centers. Some inhibition is lost, and the illusion of being stimulated occurs. But then it takes only a little more to depress the lower nervous centers, with quite a different effect, because then the drinker won't be able to function as well sexually or otherwise as he was before. The more he drinks, the longer it will take a boy to have an erection and ejaculate. As for the girl, the more she drinks, the less likely she'll be to want sex.

In the case of drugs, it must be remembered that there are two broad categories: depressants, like alcohol, and stimulants. Marijuana, for example, is a depressant, and the popular belief that "pot and sex" are inseparable companions is as much a delusion as the belief about alcohol. If a stimulant drug is taken —one of the amphetamines, or the highly dangerous methedrine, known as "speed"—the effect, paradoxically, is the same. Such drugs stimulate the individual every way but sexually and have a depressing effect on sexual behavior. "Main line" drugs like heroin knock out the taker sexually, and he or she is completely unable to perform under their influence, notwithstanding that there may be elaborate sexual fantasies.

Girls (and boys for that matter) should understand that alcohol and drugs are like crutches as far as sex is concerned. If people think they need them to have sex, then there's something wrong that can't be corrected without professional counseling. Sex exists, fully and beautifully, by itself without any artificial help.

CHAPTER 6
The Female Orgasm

Orgasms are one of those things that a good many women worry about unnecessarily. Mary McCarthy, the novelist, once called this perennial anxiety "the tyranny of the orgasm." Young girls aren't so likely to worry about it, since most of them won't experience it before they're fifteen. But they will during the next five years, one way or the other, and there should be no problems about it that healthy attitudes or good counseling can't solve.

Quite naturally, however, girls *are* curious about the orgasm. Their curiosity is stimulated by what they read. If there's a common denominator to their questions, it would be, "What is it really like? How will I feel? How do I know when I'm having it?"

Many of the greatest writers of world literature have tried to answer those questions, and of course, modern novels are full of less masterful descriptions. Doctors describe its clinical aspects, and sometimes those who specialize in sexual studies are able, in a way, to combine the two. One of the most famous of these researchers, the British sexologist Havelock Ellis, whose *Studies in the Psychology of Sex* was a pioneering landmark in the field, describes orgasm achieved by intercourse as a state in which "the individual, as a separate person, tends to disappear. He has become one with another person, as nearly one as the conditions of existence ever permit." Describing how a woman feels when she is having orgasm, Ellis speaks of her as having a "feeling of relieved tension and agreeable repose—a moment when, as one woman expresses it, together with intense pleasure, there is, as it were, a floating up into a higher sphere . . . [After the orgasm] there is a sensation of repose and self-assurance, and often an accession of free and joyous energy. . . . She may experience a feeling as of intoxication, lasting for several hours, an intoxication that is followed by no evil reaction."

Today, research into the nature of sexual response has given us a fairly comprehensive knowledge of what happens to the body during orgasm. It can be divided into four parts, of which the orgasm itself is the third. First, there is the excitement phase, beginning with a moistening of the vagina by its lubricating fluid. This moistening occurs in ten to thirty seconds from the first sexual stimulation, no matter what its source may be. Stimulation of the clitoris contributes to this phase too, although it isn't essential. The nipples on the breast come erect, and the breasts themselves increase in size. The outer lips of the vulva, the labia majora, open a little, while the inner lips also tend to swell. Aside from the sex organs, this phase is also reflected in other parts of the body, as the voluntary muscles tense, the pulse rate increases, blood pressure rises, and a rosy glow called the "sex flush" appears on the skin.

Excitement is succeeded by the plateau phase—although it would be hard to say exactly where one phase stops and the next begins. Now the rate of breathing increases, and pulse rate and blood pressure begin to rise. The sex flush becomes more marked and widespread. Muscle tension is heightened. The area around the breast nipples swells. Most dramatic, however, is the swelling of the tissues around the outer third of the vagina, so that the diameter of the opening is reduced as much as 50 percent, enabling it to grip the penis. Changes continue in the uterus and vagina, and the uterus itself is enlarged, doubling in size in women who have had children. The clitoris elevates, like a male erection, and the inner lips change in color from pink to bright red. This color change signals that the orgasm is going to occur in a minute or a minute and a half, if stimulation continues.

Orgasm itself is the third phase. There is a feeling of intense pleasure as the outer third of the vaginal tube goes into rhythmic muscular contractions that come four fifths of a second apart until the intensity tapers off. In a mild orgasm there may be only three to five contractions; in an intense one, eight to twelve. The uterus also contracts rhythmically, in wavelike motions like its contractions during childbirth, but these contractions are not felt. Other muscles may contract in the same way. In the rest of the body, pulse rate, blood pressure, and breathing rate reach their peaks, the sex flush is pronounced, and all the body's muscles respond in some way. Hands and feet contract in a spasm. Through it all, both female and male are unaware of these muscular exertions, and may be surprised when some of their muscles ache the next day.

After the orgasm, a kind of final resolution occurs. The swelling around the nipples subsides, giving an illusion that they are more erect than ever. This appearance is a sign that a woman has really experienced orgasm. The sex flush disappears rapidly, and in many females a filmy sheen of perspiration appears on the body. Within five to ten seconds the clitoris returns to its normal position, but it may take five or ten minutes or as long as a half hour to get back to normal size. The vagina relaxes too, the uterus shrinks, and the cervix descends to its normal position. At this point, the passage through the cervix enlarges, which probably makes it easier for the sperm cells to swim into the uterus. It may be as long as a half hour after orgasm before a girl's entire body returns to the state it was in before she was stimulated. If she has reached the plateau stage without experiencing orgasm, it will take much longer—an hour or even several hours.

Orgasm can be a very mild experience, almost as mild as a peaceful sigh, or it can be an extreme state of ecstasy, with much thrashing about and momentary loss of awareness. It can last for a very few seconds or for thirty seconds and longer. There is, in brief, no right or wrong way to have an orgasm.

There has long been a common misconception, still prevalent even today, that there are two different kinds of orgasm, one achieved by stimulation of the clitoris, and thus called a "clitoral orgasm," the other a "vaginal orgasm," accomplished by the penis's penetration of the vagina. The first was thought to be achieved by masturbation, petting, or intercourse if the male pubic area pressed against the clitoris. It was considered to be an immature kind of orgasm, related to early sexual experiences. The vaginal orgasm was believed to be more mature and to be the ultimate sexual experience for a woman.

Today we know these ideas aren't true, and that in intercourse it is the stimulation of the clitoris by the male area above the penis which brings on orgasm in conjunction with the pulling down of the labia by the action of the penis moving in and out of the vagina. This in turn stimulates the clitoris because the pulling-down action creates a hood of flesh over the sensitive tip of the clitoris, rubbing against it.

In fact, there is no real difference in the kind of orgasms girls have, either by masturbation, petting, or intercourse. The idea that if a girl has sex in one particular way, say masturbation, she won't be able to have orgasm in intercourse is simply not true.

Whatever its duration or intensity, the orgasm is a unique and specific enough experience so that when a girl has one, she will be in no doubt that she's having it. In a sense, it's like a much more familiar bodily function, the sneeze. After reading the description of orgasm I've just given, if a girl still has doubts about whether she's had one or not, the chances are good that she hasn't.

There are several sources of orgasm. For young girls up to fifteen, most orgasms are produced (in those who have them) by self-masturbation. I'll have more to say about that in a later chapter. Dreams are another source, but only about two girls out of a hundred achieve orgasm that way at fifteen; by twenty, this figure increases to eight out of a hundred. At fifteen, three girls out of a hundred have orgasm by petting to climax, but again a dramatic change occurs in the next five years. At twenty, nearly 25 percent of girls who have orgasm achieve it this way. Only 6 percent of girls have had orgasm from intercourse at fifteen; from sixteen to twenty, this figure rises to 11 percent. An even smaller percentage, 2 percent, have had orgasm with other girls at fifteen, and at twenty this figure has risen by only a single percentage point.

Reading this, some girls may get the idea that everybody is engaged in some kind of sexual activity all the time; and if they've never had intercourse, they may be wondering why so much fuss is made about the orgasm. After all, they reason, it may be a pleasurable experience to be enjoyed later, but they see no reason to get upset because they're not having it now. That's understandable. But there *is* something to be said for those who do have orgasm early. The longer a girl delays having it, whatever its source, the more difficult it may be to have it in later life because of the steady buildup of inhibition in the meantime.

Some parents may not like to hear such things, but it's demonstrably true that girls who have orgasm when they're young—that is, up to fifteen—are those who have the least difficulty having one later on. It doesn't matter whether the orgasm comes from intercourse, petting, or masturbation. Half the girls who have never had an orgasm before they have it in marriage or some other relationship fail to have one during the first year of that relationship, whatever it may be. Of those who *have* experienced it, only one in ten fails to have it in these circumstances of regular intimacy. Surprisingly, girls who have intercourse when they're young but don't experience orgasm have just as hard a time, or harder, having it when they're established in a regular relationship, whether it's marriage or not. Obviously, a girl who learns what orgasm is at an early point in her adolescence is going to have a more fulfilling time later on.

One superstition that needs to be discarded is the idea, earnestly believed by some people, that if a girl learns to have an orgasm by masturbating herself or having someone do it to her, she will be so accustomed to this method of achieving it that she will have trouble experiencing it in intercourse. There's no truth whatever in this notion. In fact, it's easier to transfer the way you achieve orgasm from one kind of sexual behavior to another than it is to have one in the first place.

One advantage girls have over boys where the orgasm is concerned is their ability to have many of them in succession. Some young boys are able to have three or four in relatively quick succession, with a short interval between, but they lose this ability progressively as they grow older. Many girls, on the other hand, from the time they begin to have them until the time they cease sexual activity, are able to have almost an unlimited number in succession. Not every girl does this, of course. There is tremendous variation among them, as there is in every other area of sexual activity. Some girls are satisfied with one, some can't keep themselves from having many. The statistics show that one or two girls out of every ten have more than one orgasm.

The second orgasm occurs almost immediately after the first, while the girl is still much aroused and hasn't come down from her orgasmic peak, or it can occur after she does come down, then builds up to a new peak, twenty or thirty minutes later. For some girls, these multiple orgasms may peak ten, thirty, or even fifty times in the course of one sex experience. Very often in such a long series, the peaks are smaller, but each one can be just as satisfying as it is to the woman who has only one.

In spite of all you may hear about that mythical trouble known as "nymphomania," there is nothing abnormal about having more than one orgasm or about wanting a great deal of sex. Most women could have several orgasms at a time if they really tried. People believe a "nymphomaniac" is a woman who can't be satisfied sexually, who is constantly excited and, whether she has orgasm or not, wants to have more and more sex. This notion was invented by males, and no doubt it's an exciting idea for them. But it's only an idea and doesn't actually exist in real life. My definition of a "nymphomaniac" is a woman who has a higher rate of sexual outlet than the person who calls her that—or as Kinsey put it so aptly, "A nymphomaniac is someone who has more sex than you do."

If a girl's sexual response is high and constant, there's no reason for her to worry about "nymphomania," that condition which doesn't exist. On the contrary, she should be pleased that she *is* so responsive, and she'll find that she's closer to males in her sexual response.

Another idea that needs rebuttal is the notion that it's highly desirable if both partners in the sex act have orgasm at the same time. That's fine if it happens, but it isn't that important. The intercourse will be pleasurable in any case, under ordinary circumstances. If they can't wait for each other, then the one who achieves orgasm first helps the one who's late to come to climax. It *is* important for the partner who hasn't had the orgasm to have one. That may require more intercourse or petting until it happens.

In the sex act itself, whether it's petting or intercourse, it's still necessary for each partner to be self-centered for the time being, enough to achieve orgasm, because paradoxically, this is the very thing that will bring most pleasure to the other partner.

But even if orgasm isn't achieved, it's not the end of the world, as some people think. Either partner can get a great deal of pleasure out of sex simply from the pleasure mutually given. So even though the orgasm is a highly enjoyable experience, it isn't the only good feeling a man or a woman can have from sex. The feeling of closeness, the shared pleasure, the blissful intimacy of people who love each other—all these have such definite positive values that the orgasm itself should never be viewed as a tyrant without which the whole act is meaningless.

The girl who has never had an orgasm may be disappointed because she doesn't automatically have one the first time she tries to achieve it by masturbation, petting, or intercourse. It's something like learning to play tennis or the piano. It's necessary to learn, through practice, how to build up to this peak. For some girls it's easier than for others. There are those who take months or years to learn it well. Others achieve it satisfactorily the first time they try. It's a learning process, like any other.

CHAPTER 7
Intercourse

In spite of the more liberal climate of sexual acceptance we're experiencing today, the question of whether young people should have premarital intercourse is far from settled. The country is rather sharply divided about this matter. On the one hand are the conservatives—a growing number in 1980, particularly because of the astonishing growth of fundamentalist religions—who want a return to the old, strict standards. On the other is a generation that has grown up much more permissively who believe that the question isn't *whether* but *when* teenagers should begin this kind of relating, and what they need to know about it if they do.

What you as an individual decide to do will be conditioned by several factors—parental influence, religious beliefs, personal behavior codes, peer pressure, and emotional factors. But certainly no one will dispute the fact that having intercourse will mark an important change in a young girl's life, and that she ought to have as much knowledge about what she's doing as possible. To give you that knowledge is the intent of this chapter.

My own feeling is that this question isn't nearly as important as it's made out to be. The fact of a penis entering a vagina isn't nearly as important a matter as what sort of relationship the two people involved are able to develop, including the kind of sexual adjustment they can make.

Interestingly enough, when people talk about "premarital sex" or "sex relations" or "sleeping with" someone, they usually mean premarital intercourse, but it's quite possible to have premarital sex or to sleep with someone without any intercourse whatever.

Girls and boys have different attitudes about intercourse and its meaning. To many boys it's a conquest —accomplishing something, imposing their desires on a girl, accompanied by a feeling of exaltation. Most girls don't have this feeling. Instead, they think of it as giving in, accepting, or permitting the male to become victorious. Not many at an early age are prepared to accept the feminist belief in equality; that will come later, if it does.

In earlier days these differences between males and females were so sharp in degree that a girl was expected to lie down and take whatever the male chose to give her. That's no longer true, of course. Now, if she chooses, a girl can be an equal partner in intercourse, enjoying it, taking part in it actively, being aggressive about it if she feels like it. Even with the new equality, however, it's still true that intercourse has a somewhat different meaning for a girl. Maybe it's because of the psychological feelings arising from the fact that she's the one being penetrated and the male is doing the penetrating.

A girl ought to consider the pros and cons carefully if she comes to a point where she thinks she's going to have to make up her mind about intercourse. She should consider the matter calmly, before emotion pushes her into a decision she might have been better prepared to make if she had thought about the alternatives.

Here are some reasons why a girl might think favorably of having intercourse for the first time:

1. It seems so obvious, but there are people who don't understand that the chief reason for having intercourse, aside from the desire to have a baby, is that it's one of the most delightful, exciting, and stimulating experiences a human being can know. It's no harder to understand wanting to have intercourse than it is to understand the urge to play tennis, swim, dance, ride a horse, or do anything else that gives us pleasure.

Unfortunately, this simple, straightforward reason has to be qualified by remembering that much of the pleasure will be lost if intercourse is accompanied by strong guilt feelings about it. Girls ought to be wary, too, of glorifying intercourse before they've had it. Everything they read or see on the screen or hear about from older girls leads them to believe that intercourse is the ultimate in human satisfactions, something almost indescribable. Then they have it, and often they're disappointed to find that the world doesn't necessarily stop, or the "earth move," as Hemingway put it in *For Whom the Bell Tolls*. Having anticipated vaguely so much more than the experience can give, they may be quite disillusioned and inquire, "Is this all there is to it? Is this what the shouting is about?" It may seem no more to such girls than a feeling like that of masturbation, only heightened by the presence of another person.

Girls who are more reasonable in their expectations are more likely to find intercourse enjoyable. The trouble is that because so much of society (and especially parents) get upset about the idea of premarital intercourse, girls who have never had it get the idea that it must be incredibly wonderful if it's so forbidden. Intercourse, however, is an important and permanent part of most people's lives. It's a wise idea to get it into perspective from the beginning.

2. For those who plan on marriage eventually, early intercourse can also be a training ground. Those who have it get some valuable lessons in learning to live with someone else in what Bernard Shaw called "the dreadful intimacy of marriage." The lessons are valuable, that is, if intercourse is performed with good techniques, if it's meaningful to the people involved, if it's part of a whole relationship, and if it's done without feelings of guilt and fear. What is done badly, however, may be carried over into marriage. It's somewhat like learning to play tennis and discovering when

95

you face someone across the net in your first real match that you haven't learned the fundamentals properly.

3. Another reason for intercourse is the fact that, unlike masturbation, it means interaction with another human being, and consequently it's a means of learning how to live with people, something everyone has to do. Because that is true, it's important that intercourse be a giving-and-receiving act.

There are many girls who regret after marriage that they didn't have premarital intercourse, because they've come to realize what a long, slow learning process it can often be after marriage. Sometimes, too late, they and their husbands discover that they're not suited to each other sexually.

As many as 80 percent of girls say the reason they didn't have more intercourse before marriage was because of strong moral objections, and another 9 percent had slight moral objections that prevented them. Nearly half admit they didn't have more because they were just not interested, while 45 percent were afraid of getting pregnant and the same percentage were afraid of public opinion. Fear of venereal disease accounted for the restraint of only 14 percent, and 22 percent say they would have had more if they had only had more opportunity.

4. If early intercourse is with a boy a girl expects to marry, it's a good way for her to find out if she's going to enjoy the constant intimacy of the bedroom with that particular young man, and of course it gives

him the same opportunity. But whatever kind of relationship she expects to establish, whether marriage or not, she'll quickly discover whether she and her partner are completely suited to each other. Sometimes people are suited in every way *except* sexually. If marriage is the end result and this discovery isn't made until after the ceremony, the result can only be eventual divorce if the difficulties are not resolved either by communication or with the help of counseling. The first times have to be a fair test, however, with the intercourse taking place in the most relaxed atmosphere. If it's done with strong guilt feelings, or done furtively and hastily, it isn't like marriage or any other kind of lasting relationship, and so it isn't a fair test.

5. People learn more easily when they're young. If the learning is correct from the beginning, sexual adjustment in marriage is made much more easily.

6. Some girls rush into intercourse because their friends are having it and they think they will lose status in the group if they don't. That's powerful pressure, but it's the worst reason for beginning intercourse.

What are the cons, then?

1. First, and most obvious, the danger of pregnancy. That danger isn't what it used to be, now that girls have access in most cases to the pill, as we now familiarly call it. But we're not out of the woods with contraceptives yet, as everyone thought when the pill was introduced. Some girls have undesirable side effects from it and have to resort to other means, and there are some doctors who refuse to prescribe it because of

evidence that it may have long-range effects on health. This is not established, however. I'll have more to say about all this a little later. For now, it's enough to say that if a proper contraceptive is available and is used properly, the possibility of pregnancy is virtually eliminated.

2. Another danger is venereal disease, a subject I'll also talk about later. Again, we don't have quite the freedom from this danger we thought we had when modern drugs like penicillin were introduced.

3. Premarital intercourse sometimes results in a forced marriage, and that's usually a poor way to enter the married state. Some people might have married each other in any case, but more often the girl (or boy) who has been compelled to marry has a more difficult time making the marriage work, and the rate of failure is high.

4. If there is guilt, there's likely to be damage of some kind, and in my opinion, this is the most important reason for not having early intercourse. Guilt is determined by the attitude each person has toward the act, and it's better not to have intercourse at all if one or both persons feel extremely guilty and are likely to suffer attacks of conscience afterward.

5. Girls are often afraid a boy will lose respect for them if they have intercourse with him, and no doubt that sometimes happens, although more often it's not so much a loss of respect as it is the boy's chalking up that conquest and moving on to the next girl, to the hurt and bewilderment of the first girl. A girl ought to

ask herself if she honestly believes a boy is more concerned about her as an individual, as a whole person, than he is with one particular part of her, the vagina. The question of virginity is sometimes involved here too—another subject I'll get to presently.

6. Guilt about early intercourse is often the result of fear about what happens to those who get caught. The worst that can happen is public knowledge and disapproval from school, parents, clergy, police, relatives, even friends. People aren't often caught, however, and if they are, how they feel about it depends a great deal on who catches them. The worst, naturally, is to have disapproving parents find out. If it's a friend or someone their own age, the result is usually no more than feelings of embarrassment.

In short, responsible boys and girls who have thought about the pros and cons and then decided to have intercourse have to accept the risks that may be involved. But just as they learn to drive defensively in high school driving classes, they should minimize the risks in a realistic way.

7. One very real danger is the possibility that the physical side of a relationship may be overemphasized. If that seems probable, the girl would be better off not to have it. The value of early sex is that it becomes an important part of a whole relationship between people, not an isolated experience. If a girl thinks a boy only wants to "make out" with her in this sense rather than have a whole relationship, she may discover that she has a sexual partner but not a friend.

8. It shouldn't be overlooked that to many people, and probably to more girls than boys, intercourse without marriage is morally wrong—and in this era when so many young people embrace fundamentalist religious faiths, that view is becoming more prevalent. In the past it was thought to be wrong for girls, but people winked at the behavior of boys; the double standard was fully established. But the new move toward equality of the sexes means that girls are entitled to equal responsibilities and opportunities in sexual as well as other areas of living. Something that's morally wrong for a girl ought to be just as wrong for a boy.

In the end the problem of early sex, whether it's premarital or just early, comes down to a question of how a girl feels about it, whether she thinks it's right or wrong. When a girl thinks it's wrong, none of the reasons for having it I've mentioned will make the slightest difference to her. If she believes it's not wrong, her responsibility then is to think carefully about the time, the place, and the partner. There's always the danger that, because the sex impulse is so powerful, a girl will simply be carried away without assessing rights or wrongs, or without being as sure as she can be about her partner's attitudes. Being forewarned by the information given here is being forearmed.

Often today it's not so much a question of whether it's going to happen early, as I've said, but *when*, and that can be an important question. The best answer is that girls shouldn't begin intercourse until they feel that they're ready for it and can handle it, with all its implications. Some reach this stage very early, some much later, and setting an arbitrary age makes no sense.

But let's assume now that the decision has been made to have it. Quite often a girl doesn't know exactly what to expect or what to do, and then the experience can be a fumbling and unsatisfactory one. For instance, if she's never seen an erect male penis, she may be frightened by the thought of such a large object penetrating her and wonder how it's possible. But as I noted in Chapter 2, what seems like a mere slit at the opening of the vagina is actually an opening of amazing flexibility, as it would have to be to make the birth of a baby possible. Remembering that will take away the fear of its being stretched painfully by the relatively small mass of a penis. Moreover, when a girl is aroused, the lubrication of the vagina that results makes insertion of the penis easy. Intercourse is more comfortable, consequently, when it's been preceded by sex play.

As for intercourse itself, the traditional position for it in our culture has the girl lying on her back with her legs apart while the boy lies on her, face to face, with his legs together. A girl sometimes will help him to insert his penis, but more often he will do it by himself. Usually the insertion is made gradually, with small thrusts forward.

If a girl is a virgin, the hymen will be broken by the penetration, with a quick, sharp twinge of pain that is soon over and sometimes but not always a little bleeding, which quickly dries up. That's the usual way of things. If the hymen happens to be tougher and the boy has to push with more force to break it, there may be a little more pain and discomfort, and possibly a girl may not enjoy this first intercourse for that reason. Its satisfactions will come in succeeding intercourse. The danger is that a girl who is unprepared for this possibility may find sex distasteful and take a long time to get over the unpleasantness of the first experience.

These days, however, many girls have their hymens broken before they ever have intercourse, either through exercise and sports or by masturbation. In any case, whatever psychological damage may be possible can be prevented, or at least minimized, if a boy pets a girl a good deal first and inserts his fingers in her vagina.

Once penetrated, the vagina clasps the penis in a velvet grip and intercourse continues with a series of pelvic thrusts. These increase in speed, frequency, and force as excitement mounts and the act moves toward orgasm, as I described earlier.

Sometimes the male ejaculates too quickly, before a girl can have her own orgasm. There are measures a boy can take for himself to prevent this, but what a girl can do in her own behalf is to slow down her partner by insisting on more petting before penetration begins, so that she will be further along the road toward orgasm.

There are other positions for intercourse, employed either for the sake of variety or because it helps the male to slow down and the female to speed up. This is best accomplished by the position in which the female lies on top of the male, with her legs together between his, or vice versa. She can help the male, and help herself, by having him put his hands on her buttocks, which pushes her pelvic area toward his and makes it easier for her to thrust and build up tension for the orgasm. The weight of her body also reduces the body movement and that, too, will help him delay ejaculation.

In another position, the couple lie on their sides facing each other, with the girl's leg often thrown over the male's leg, permitting them to get closer together. In fact, people can have intercourse sitting down or standing up as well, but these positions are taken more for the sake of variety.

Still another position is what is commonly called "dog fashion"—some prefer to call it "doggie"—in which the girl lies on her stomach with the male over her, or on her side with him behind her, or on her back with the male beneath her. An advantage to this position is that it makes the clitoris more available for stimulation with the hand.

If a girl thinks some of these positions are strange, she should know, for example, that people who live in some South Sea islands have a position that seems truly odd to us, in which the female lies on her back with her legs out, while the male kneels or squats in front of her to make his pelvic thrusts. There are, in fact, many ways to have intercourse and there isn't any "right" or "wrong" about it. "Right" is what works best for the people involved, and what may seem strange to one couple is commonplace for another. Nor is there any such thing as a "normal" position. Many people in our culture think the position in which the female lies on her back is the "normal" one, but it's only the most common.

When intercourse is over, there's another difference between males and females. The male usually feels immediately let down and wants to withdraw and go to sleep, while the female may want more penetration and more love play. She appreciates the man who understands this and thinks of her different kind of need. A knowledgeable girl can explain this to a boy who may not know about it.

A girl (or a boy) who wants to get out of bed immediately after intercourse and wash herself is probably reflecting another attitude about sex—the feeling that it's something dirty. Most likely she's not really happy about the act itself, but there's nothing unclean about the body's secretions.

Love, or at least affection, is the motivation to intercourse for most girls, and so it's no wonder that they're curious about those who do it for money. Young girls often regard prostitutes with mingled fascination and horror. They find it hard to understand how a woman could have intercourse with just *any* man. In prostitution, affection, friendship, or the interchange of feelings don't often occur. Sometimes there is hostility involved in these encounters, on one or both sides, and sometimes it turns out to be a depressing experience for a man. For the prostitute, the act may be only an expression of her hatred for men, although, contrary to popular belief, she may actually enjoy sex with many different men and will have orgasm with some of them.

The contrast, however, is striking. Prostitution is often a sex act performed in a drab room somewhere, in a rooming house or a fourth-class hotel, and the sordid setting often reflects the nature of the act. The same lack of emotional content may exist, nevertheless, if the prostitute is being paid a hundred dollars or more, and the act takes place in an expensive hotel or apartment. What's important is the fact that, even when intercourse takes place between people who have only warm feelings for each other, the quality of the act may be affected by the setting. This aspect of it should be emphasized, because it's much more important for a girl not to be interrupted or found out than it is for a boy.

Couples who have made a decision to have intercourse need to exercise their ingenuity in finding the best place to have it, where the chance of being discovered will not be great. One of the more common places, but one that can be cramped and uncomfortable, is a car parked along the road. Another is some secluded spot, where there is also the danger of robbery or rape or being found by people who get sexual pleasure out of creeping up on parked cars. The home of either the boy or the girl is possible only if they can be absolutely sure that parents won't return home unexpectedly. If there's any doubt, anxiety and tension will almost inevitably surround the act. Motel and hotel rooms aren't usually accessible to younger couples. In the end, it seems, places like woods, a beach, or a secluded area one can walk to are likely to work out better than any of the others I've mentioned.

I don't want to minimize the importance of the step a girl takes when she decides to have intercourse for the first time. It's her crossing of the Rubicon, from which there is no turning back. While it's true that large parts of our society make too much out of it, at the same time it must be remembered that it's one of the most important steps in a girl's life. The fundamental fact is that once she's had intercourse she will never again be a virgin, whether her hymen has been broken beforehand or not. But then, virginity or non-virginity is more a state of mind than it is a condition of the body.

For example, here's a fifteen-year-old girl who is warm, open, affectionate, and hasn't developed any guilt feelings about sex. In the course of a long relationship with a boyfriend, during which there has been an increased emotional involvement with each other, along with increased petting experience, intercourse occurs at some particular point. In this girl's mind there has been no sudden or dramatic change in her status from being a virgin to being a nonvirgin. Instead, the intercourse has been only another expression of her fondness for the boy. If the relationship is broken off later and she begins a new relationship with another boy, she will not enter it with any different feelings toward herself than she had in her previous relationship.

Even though intercourse may not be the big deal it's so often made out to be, it does provide a certain completeness to a relationship. If people feel open and loving toward each other, yet erect certain barriers— no petting below the waist, or everything but intercourse—a certain restraint is bound to develop. I'm not suggesting that there be no barriers. I'm only saying that it's better to face these barriers consciously and understand the pros and cons of erecting them. In sex, as in every other aspect of human relationships, understanding is the glue that holds everything together.

CHAPTER 8
Consequences

The most obvious consequence of intercourse is pregnancy. It isn't quite the problem it once was, as I've noted, because contraceptives are now widely available to girls, at least those who can afford to buy them; and if pregnancy does occur, abortion is available by virtue of a Supreme Court ruling, and it is no longer the dangerous, back-alley deal it used to be—unless its opponents succeed in changing or circumventing the law. Still, the number of teenage pregnancies remains a social problem, disturbing to careers and life prospects, and it's one not easily solved. Moralists think it can be solved simply by forbidding girls to have intercourse, but anyone familiar with everyday teenage life knows how futile that is.

It's easy enough for people to condemn the pregnant teenager, and some do, but it's a far more constructive thing to help her. Some school systems in urban centers help by setting up classes especially for pregnant girls, enabling them to continue their schooling and giving them instruction in prenatal and maternal care, with excellent results.

For all the obvious reasons, however, it's better to

prevent pregnancy if possible. Since the early days of mankind, attempts have been made to avoid it by using some kind of contraceptive device. We've come a long way down that particular medical road, and there is now available a wide choice of contraceptive means, although their usefulness and practicality where young girls are concerned are not always satisfactory. There isn't one that doesn't have some kind of controversy surrounding it. Let's consider them one by one.

Withdrawal is probably the one most commonly used by young people, or at least those who don't have the money, opportunity, or motivation to practice mechanical means. Withdrawal before ejaculation sounds simple and easy, and of course it doesn't require any apparatus, but it's not so easy as it sounds, unfortunately. In the first place, it's not so enjoyable, because at the height of sexual excitement, when both people are most involved with the act and the boy wants to push in, he'll have to pull out instead. Sometimes his excitement will be so great he won't be able to stop at all, but even if he's successful in doing so, there may be enough sperm in the lubricating fluid that comes out of his penis before he ejaculates to make a girl pregnant. It's also possible for a male to ejaculate at the opening of the vagina, and even though the girl may still have her hymen intact, sperm can find their way through it and move all the way up the length of the vagina into the uterus. Consequently, withdrawal is not only unsatisfactory at best, but it's also unsafe. No wonder we hear it said that the biggest lie a boy can tell a girl is, "Don't worry, I won't get you pregnant. I won't come inside you."

Another method is to avoid having intercourse when the egg is in the process of coming out of the ovary and down into the Fallopian tubes. If we could be absolutely sure when that was happening, pregnancy could be avoided successfully by not having intercourse during the few hours of the month when this process occurs. But the problem is to be sure. If a girl kept an accurate record of her menstrual periods, the process could be pinpointed at fourteen days before she began the next menstruation. That would be accurate, however, only if she had regular periods, which many girls do not, and if she ovulated only once a month. Some girls ovulate more than once a month.

Nevertheless, many people attempt to use this method because it's the only one approved by the Roman Catholic Church. The "rhythm method," as it's called, is uncertain and I wouldn't recommend it if people don't want a baby. If a couple isn't too concerned about whether they have one or not, it can be regarded as a somewhat half-hearted method of contraception, which is often not successful.

Another method is to put a rubber sheath over the penis to catch the semen and prevent the sperm from going into the uterus—a method that is centuries old; silk handkerchiefs or other fabrics were used before rubber was invented. This sheath is called a condom or a safety or a rubber—to run down a list nearly everyone knows—and it can be bought at drugstores or, in many states, from vending machines at filling stations and elsewhere. Condoms are relatively cheap (although in 1980 they were going up, like everything else in an inflationary world), and are ordinarily used only once. The quality of condoms has improved a great deal since the Second World War, and there is rarely any breakage or pinholes that might permit semen to ooze through. Although federal law requires only every tenth one to be inspected, the companies that make them inspect each one.

Still, some simple precautions are wise. For example, it's a bad idea to carry condoms around for a long time without using them—say three months or more —especially if the package is open to the air, because rubber deteriorates. You'd better be sure the boy you may be planning to have intercourse with knows that. And *you* should know that occasionally one will slip off the penis during intercourse. Condoms aren't 100 percent safe, but they're about 99 percent effective, and they are the best contraceptive available, with the possible exception of the pill, which we'll talk about later.

Substitutes for condoms should never be used, even though a friend may recommend one. Some boys make crude and ineffective attempts to manufacture condoms out of rubber balloons or even Saran Wrap. These devices are little better than no protection at all.

Another method of contraception is for the girl to wash out her vagina with water containing some antiseptic after intercourse. This is known as a douche (pronounced *doosh*), a French word. Douching requires a douche bag, an apparatus that looks like a hot-water bottle with a tube; it forces water into the vagina. Since it's an unwieldy thing to carry around, few younger girls will be likely to have one. This fact has led to some unusual substitutes, such as taking a Coke bottle, shaking it up, and squirting it into the vagina by placing the thumb partly over the top. By any technique, especially this one, the douche is a very poor and ineffective method of contraception, and a large number of pregnancies result from reliance on it. Some antiseptics can even burn or irritate the vagina.

Still another contraceptive technique, much more in use among married women than among young girls until recently, is a dome-shaped vaginal cap made of rubber; it must be fitted by a doctor, since they come in different sizes to accommodate the varying sizes of women. This cap, known as a "diaphragm," fits over the cervix, closing off the entrance to the uterus so the sperm can't enter. As I've said, it must be fitted by a doctor to be sure the size is right, and then a girl or woman must learn to put it in herself before intercourse, must use a special cream or jelly with it, and must leave it in for eight hours afterward. Few young girls used this device until recently, since many doctors were unwilling to fit those who were unmarried, but not many physicians these days will make such a moral judgment unless they have strong religious convictions. Some may require parental consent, but if a girl has a good relationship with her doctor, especially if the physician is female, she will encounter no problems. She also has the right to change doctors if she isn't satisfied with the one she has.

Some women also use foams, creams, jellies, suppositories, or tablets, all available at drugstores, instead of the diaphragm. None of these has proved to be as safe as the condom, and most girls don't want to use them in any case, for esthetic reasons.

During the past few years an oral contraceptive, now known popularly as "the pill," has been developed. A girl must take these pills, one a day, for twenty-one days, and then stop in order to menstruate. Although the pills are constantly being refined, there are still possible side effects, like feeling sick or putting on weight, so that it's necessary for a doctor to prescribe this method and to watch his patient for a few months to see what effect the pills have on her and whether she's affected more by one kind than another. Some doctors have raised more serious questions about the effects of the pill, and there are some who refuse to prescribe them. In general, the rare side effects seem to depend on the girl; some react and some don't. The long-range dangers, if they exist, are still the subject of study, and girls who fear taking the chance should probably not be taking the pill because such anxiety connected with intercourse is surely not a good thing.

Use of these pills has somewhat leveled off, but in any case, few girls of very young ages will be likely to use them, for obvious reasons. However, in spite of continuing controversy, many doctors still believe the pill is the best method of contraception we currently have. The girl who uses it properly doesn't need to worry about getting pregnant; when they fail, the failure is nearly always the result of human error—carelessness about taking them.

There is also the intrauterine device, commonly called "the IUD," made of plastic, which comes in several different shapes and is inserted into the uterus by a doctor and left there for months or even years. For a time this method was considered by many doctors to be ideal, since it was easy to insert (although a physician had to do it), and was virtually guaranteed to prevent pregnancy. The drawback was that not every woman who hadn't had a child could use it. More recently, however, serious questions have been raised about the IUD's safety. Girls who have multiple sexual partners and use an IUD are more likely to develop pelvic inflammation. There is much less enthusiasm for it these days on the part of physicians, some of whom continue to prescribe it, however.

Contraception can be the responsibility of either the male or the female. Withdrawal and the condom are the techniques the male uses, until a "pill" for men is developed, which may not be far away. All the others are methods for the female to use. For young couples, the best available device is still the condom, which places considerable responsibility in the hands of the boy.

There's another aspect of the matter too. Girls in general have a more romantic concept of sex and intercourse than boys, and consequently many of them have no conscious intention of having intercourse but get carried away by the mood of the moment and the situation, and they have it without any thought of contraception. Thus, any planning about whether a boy has a condom on before intercourse runs against the natural inclinations of the girl. For most of them, such planning ahead takes away a good part of the pleasure of intercourse. They want it to be spontaneous and uninterrupted mechanically.

For that reason, many girls are averse also to using the vaginal foams, jellies, and suppositories that are available in drugstores without a doctor's prescription. They're easy to use and relatively inexpensive, and they're more dependable than they were, but some girls are dismayed, for example, when the little almond-shaped suppositories don't melt when they should or don't melt completely. Or else they melt too easily, and girls think it's too messy to insert them. They *must* melt, however, because it's the chemicals they contain, coating the vagina, that kill the sperm. Similarly, it's the cream that does the job when used with the diaphragm, since this rubber cap only holds the cream in place against the opening of the uterus.

All these devices have to be inserted into the vagina just before intercourse, and some girls think this is a messy business. The cream may also leak out next day in the form of a discharge. Foams, however, disappear during intercourse and have no odor, but they still have to be applied with an applicator. Girls anticipating intercourse who insert the foam several hours before they think they're going to have it are taking a chance; the interval should be no longer than an hour.

I can understand the feelings girls have about these mechanical and possibly "messy" devices, but at the same time I can only say that the surest way to get pregnant is to be overcome by the excitement and romance of the moment without regard for the outcome and without doing something about the consequences. We have so many teenage pregnancies, not because the devices fail, but because they're used improperly or not at all.

But let's assume now that, whatever the reason, a girl does become pregnant. The first indication will be the missing of a menstrual period, and pregnancy will then be confirmed by testing. She has four options open to her. She can get married, but usually that's a poor choice because both boy and girl are likely to be too young to start family life. Few boys can support a girl at that age, and it means that schooling will probably be interrupted or even ended for both of them. Marriages begun under such circumstances are usually not as successful as those that are made because the couple wanted to marry.

The second option is to have the baby without marrying the boy. Again, this may not be a good choice because the girl is usually not able to support the baby herself and give it the proper environment. If she has to quit school and go to work, relying on her mother or day-care centers to take the child during working hours, she's still likely to have a great many emotional and economic problems.

A third option is to have the baby but have it adopted immediately. There are numerous complications here. The girl may have to be able to leave her community for five or six months, in most cases, and keep the matter a secret. Again, many girls who go through the nine months of pregnancy and birth don't want to give up the baby, no matter how sensible it may be to do so. Putting a baby up for adoption is a painful process at best.

The fourth option is abortion. While this operation is legal, as I've said, there will be complications if the girl is religious herself or comes from a religious family, especially if she's a Catholic. The Catholic faith believes as a matter of doctrine that the soul enters the fetus at the moment of conception, and so opposes abortion, as do other "right-to-life" advocates, who consider abortion the same as murder.

Nevertheless, a good many girls and women do have abortions, which are relatively easy to obtain from thoroughly qualified doctors and under the best conditions. If done properly, by a qualified physician in an office or hospital, it's safer than a tonsillectomy. It can only be dangerous in the hands of incompetent doctors or abortionists who aren't even doctors and work under unsterile conditions. Infection or death may result in such circumstances. An infected abortion can mean that a girl will not be able to get pregnant again during her lifetime.

If a girl thinks she is pregnant, the first thing she should do is to make certain she is. This is done by means of a medical test that uses either a blood sample or a sample of urine. The laboratory test is relatively inexpensive and is obtained through a physician. At least two other tests, possibly less reliable, are available over the counter at drugstores.

Once pregnancy is established, the best advice that can be given is to do what I'm sure most girls would dread most. Nevertheless, it is her parents she should turn to first for help. It's true that there are many parents who will give their daughter a rough time and in general treat her shabbily if she becomes pregnant without being married, but, on the other hand, there are many others who prove to be warm, loving, and protective in this situation. Naturally, they will probably blame the boy and be angry with him, but that's only to be expected.

Sometimes there are other adults in the community a girl can turn to, especially her doctor; sometimes it's a clergyman, or, more likely, an adult in the family to whom she feels especially close, possibly an aunt or uncle or an older, married sister.

If abortion is the option decided upon, remember that it should be done before the end of the third month because the fetus is large enough after that to make the operation more difficult.

One thing to be avoided absolutely is reliance on

self-administered drugs or some other means of bringing on a miscarriage, which loosens the fetus from the uterine walls and lets it slip down into the vagina and out of the body. The drugs popularly believed to cause miscarriage—quinine, castor oil, ergot, among others—almost never do. If they do, it's only in cases where the girl would have had the miscarriage in any case. About one in eight pregnancies ends in miscarriage in the ordinary course of events. However, if a girl is afraid she might become pregnant, she can get pills (or an injection) from her doctor if she sees him immediately (no later than the next day) after intercourse. This medication is often effective in stopping pregnancy.

Even worse is to try to induce abortion by some means like falling on the stomach, inserting something into the uterus, or jumping from a chair or table to jar the fetus loose. These are extremely dangerous practices. They often lead to injury, infection, or death, and even if they were likely to work, the danger would be far too great.

Pregnancy, however, is not the only possible consequence of intercourse. Venereal diseases are transmitted only by some sort of sexual contact, and that danger is present too.

There are several kinds of venereal disease, but the two most common are gonorrhea and syphilis. The symptoms are the same for girls as for boys, by and large, but because the girl's sex organs are more hidden, they will be more difficult to spot. In gonorrhea, for example, a boy notices a burning in his penis when he urinates, a symptom appearing eight to fifteen days after he is infected. A little later, pus with a characteristic and rather unpleasant odor begins to drip from the penis. Girls, on the other hand, will have a painful irritation in the lining of the urethra and it, too, produces pus; but since the secretion is not so easily noticed as in boys, a girl may think she has nothing more than a vaginal infection.

In syphilis, a more serious matter, the germ invades the body through any mucous membrane. In the girl, this can be the vagina or the mouth. The first symptom is a single sore, not painful, followed by a rash, which may appear on any part of the body. It is a light rash, lasting for only a short time, and so may go unnoticed. The sore appears most often on the penis of the boy or the vaginal lips of the girl. It appears about sixty days after the infection and goes away in time. If the disease is not treated, however, it continues to fester in the body silently, although it may seem to disappear entirely and not return for months or even years. When it does return, it will be in a much more violent state, able to do serious damage to body organs, and eventually, if unchecked, may even result in death.

A girl develops the same characteristic syphilitic sore, or chancre, as the boy, but it may be hidden in the vagina or the mouth so that she may not know she has it. There is, incidentally, no truth to the common superstition that you can tell if a girl has venereal disease by pouring whiskey or Coke on her sex organ, and if it burns, she's infected. The only way a girl can tell is if she has a visible chancre on the lips of her vagina or has a discharge of pus from the vagina or urethra.

Venereal disease is not the scourge it used to be, fortunately. Gonorrhea once could be cured only by long and sometimes painful treatment, if it was cured at all. Syphilis ran rampant through the world, unchecked for centuries, and even in modern times it has been called "the great killer." But the discovery of penicillin and the sulfa drugs has brought these diseases under control. Like any other controllable disease, however, individual cases must be indentified and treated, particularly now, when resistant strains of the germs are appearing. That's why it's important not to treat VD lightly; don't listen to anyone who repeats the old cliché, "It's no worse than a bad cold." Without treatment, the consequences are far worse than a bad cold's and, in the case of syphilis, can be fatal.

A girl who has any symptoms of venereal disease, or thinks she has, should consult the doctor. Young girls and boys are likely to be afraid that he (or she) will tell their parents if they do have it, but most doctors respect the confidential nature of the relationship between doctor and patient, even if it's a family doctor who may have delivered his (or her) patient. Nevertheless, the doctor is required by law to report the case to the local board of health, although not all physicians do so. Unquestionably there are a great many unreported cases. The board of health is interested in only one thing. It wants to know where the girl or boy got the disease; it has the authority to ask them whom they have been having intercourse with and will examine these persons to see where the infection originated. This is embarrassing, but there is no other way to lower the VD rate. It should be emphasized, too, that the board of health is not concerned with moral aspects. It doesn't seek to condemn people or expose them; it wants only to track down the source of infection. Consequently, identity is protected.

Penicillin shots are the treatment for both syphilis and gonorrhea. The series lasts for about five days and is almost always effective. We're fortunate to have a cure for these diseases that's quick and simple. If everyone cooperates with the board of health by letting them know when the disease appears and with whom the exposure took place, both ailments can be cured in most cases, and we'll be able to keep VD under control.

There are two other lesser-known venereal diseases you should know about. One is called NGU, meaning non-gonococcal urethritis. It is now the most prevalent venereal disease, and probably the most common sexually transmitted disease. It was considered to be only a minor problem until recently, when it was discovered that it could cause lifelong sterility in men and women if not treated. Some specialists believe that one variety of NGU bacteria is possibly more dangerous than gonococcus. Since most girls and women don't have symptoms that indicate the presence of NGU and so become carriers without knowing it, and since cases aren't usually reported to health officials, as gonorrhea and syphilis are, it has spread rapidly until it now affects more than two million people a year. While it doesn't usually respond to penicillin, other antibiotics are effective. You should see your doctor if you notice anything unusual such as pain or a discharge in your genital area.

The other venereal disease that is not so well known as the others is the result of an invasion by the germs called herpes simplex—the same ones that cause cold sores. They can spread through sexual contact and the result is an extremely painful infection of the genitals in both men and women. It isn't fatal, of course, or damaging to organs, but it's enough to put those who have it out of the running for some time, and it's not pleasant to have. At the moment, no cure is available, and unfortunately the disease tends to recur.

Whatever the consequences of intercourse may be, and I've covered the most important ones here, the best advice I can give any girl is to learn about these consequences before she makes any decisions about whether to have intercourse. If she possesses the knowledge beforehand, she will not only be far better able to make a decision, but the consequences, if they come, will not be unexpected. Beyond that, the most difficult consequences of intercourse for most girls to handle are the feelings of fear or guilt, or both, that the act may inspire. Since these factors are the enemy of any meaningful human relationship, a girl who finds that she can't handle these feelings would be better off not to have intercourse at all, and thus avoid the struggle over consequences entirely.

But even if there's no fear or guilt, and even if a girl has weighed her decision carefully before taking so important a step (and unfortunately, that isn't very common), intercourse may produce unforeseen psychological consequences. A girl may feel that, after all, she is not ready for such a relationship, or that she has created a situation that disturbs and upsets the way she wants to live. Sometimes, in a moment of regret, she may feel that she has given herself away too easily—for no more than a quick sensation. It's not uncommon, too, for her to see her partner in a different light, and to be disappointed in him as a human being.

Obviously, as all these consequences indicate, intercourse isn't a matter to be taken lightly or casually. It demands much more than a physical response.

CHAPTER 9
Masturbation

Masturbation has been defined in several ways, but the definition I prefer calls it "a deliberate self-stimulation which results in sexual arousal." There are those, however, who think of self-masturbation in a much broader way. They regard it as any kind of self-stimulation that gives pleasure, a definition broad enough to include rubbing the nose and riding on a roller coaster.

Public attitudes about masturbation stem from the Judeo-Christian religious tradition. The founders of these faiths believed that sex must be only for the purpose of procreation, and because masturbation does not result in pregnancy, organized religions have always been against it.

Today these attitudes are gradually changing. Even the churches, or at least some of them, now look upon sex as something pleasurable in its own right. But taboos that have existed for centuries are not so easily changed, and there are still a great many adults, including parents, who are against masturbation, even though they might not be able to say exactly why. If they read the teachings of Freud and his followers, they find some justification for their views, because Freud said, in effect, that masturbation might be all right for young children, when it was part of growing up, but it was childish, immature, and undesirable for older people.

It isn't surprising, then, that girls are often influenced by negative attitudes and, when they masturbate, find that they feel guilty about it. That's unfortunate because, if they allow these ancient social taboos to interfere, they won't get all the pleasure that's possible out of masturbation. The truth is that masturbation is only a part of ordinary sexual activity, like petting or intercourse, and there's no more reason to feel guilty about it than about anything else we do sexually as human beings. Doing it becomes a problem only if a girl's own code or her religion tell her that sex is just for procreation and so it's morally wrong to masturbate, or if she happens to feel that when parents or other respected adults are against it, she must conform to their attitudes. If such a girl masturbates in spite of strong moral feelings against it, she'll probably find that it does her more harm than good, in a strictly psychological sense.

Some people, even doctors, have argued that masturbation is harmful because it fixates a girl at that level and makes it difficult or impossible for her to enjoy intercourse. But there's no truth in this argument, as I've said earlier. In fact, studies show that girls who learn to have orgasm through masturbation have an *easier* time in responding to intercourse than those who don't. It's also said that masturbation does all kinds of physical harm to young girls, but there's no truth in that either. No one believes anymore that masturbation causes facial pimples, poor posture, dullness of mind, cancer, stomach upsets, sterility, headaches, and kidney trouble. No medical evidence exists that shows any kind of relationship between masturbation and illness.

If any physical harm at all comes from masturbation, it's an occasional local irritation caused by a great deal of friction, or an occasional minor infection caused by the insertion of some unclean object into the vagina or the urethra.

On the other hand, there are many reasons why masturbation is beneficial. First, it brings a great deal of pleasure to a girl, especially if she masturbates to the point of orgasm. It's also pleasurable without orgasm, but stopping short may leave her momentarily frustrated and uneasy, with a good deal of congestion in her genitals, which may be uncomfortable but otherwise is nothing to worry about.

Masturbation also teaches a girl how to have an orgasm, and it does so in the most simple, direct way possible, so that it will be easier for her to have orgasm when she does have intercourse. Another good reason for masturbation is the fact that it's easily available as long as there's privacy. It permits a girl to learn how her own body reacts and allows her to experiment with herself so that she can more easily teach someone else the things that make her feel good sexually. Then, too, there's no danger of venereal disease or of pregnancy. Masturbation does no harm to a girl, or to anyone else; it offers a variety of sexual experience; and it provides a way to develop a fantasy life, an important part of human sexuality.

There's a sharp contrast between boys and girls where masturbation is concerned. Kinsey's figures showed that, by the age of fifteen, about 25 percent of girls had masturbated to the point of orgasm, while the figure for boys was virtually 100 percent. There is reason to believe the figure for girls would have to be revised upward today, with the spread of knowledge, generally greater sexual freedom, and the impetus provided by the women's movement. Eventually more than 60 percent of women masturbate, but much of it occurs in later years, even in marriage. For young girls, the average frequency of masturbation was about once every two or three weeks, according to Kinsey, but that figure may have moved upward too. In any case, there is a great deal of variation. Some girls do it many times a week, others very infrequently.

Most boys learn how to masturbate by hearing about it from other boys, but most girls discover it for themselves. Again, this reflects the fact that boys do much more talking about sex among themselves than girls do. As many as a quarter of the girls who don't begin masturbating until they're in their early twenties or older still discover it by themselves. Oddly enough, some girls masturbate for a long time before they realize that this is what they're doing.

Girls also learn about it from books like this one, or from other books, or from other girls or boys. Less than half the girls learn about it that way, but it's how three fourths of the boys find out. About one girl in every ten learns of masturbation as the result of petting, and about the same number through seeing someone else do it. Only about 3 percent of girls learn through a lesbian experience; the figure is much higher for boys. Surprisingly, there are still many girls who don't know it's possible to masturbate.

However it's learned, the techniques are the same, and they center on stimulation of the clitoris. Most girls masturbate by rubbing the clitoris or the part of the vulva immediately around it. The girl usually moves a finger or several fingers or perhaps her whole hand gently and rhythmically over this section, sometimes applying steady and increased pressure as she builds toward orgasm. She may also use the heel of her foot or some other object placed against this area. Some girls find that only a gentle pressure is all that's needed, while others need to apply so much pressure that it takes one hand on top of another to accomplish it. This way of masturbating is usually done while the girl is lying on her back or perhaps sitting up, but it's also done while lying on the stomach, with one hand underneath placed over the vulva and a finger manipulating the clitoris. There are girls who like to lie on their stomachs and place bunched-up sheets or a blanket between their legs, rubbing against it to attain orgasm. Others like to rub themselves against objects—stuffed animals in bed, for example, or furniture in the room, like the arm of a chair.

There are a great many ways for a girl to masturbate —more than a boy enjoys. Some girls like to do it in the bathtub, using the stream from a faucet directed against the clitoris, or a needle shower. Others learn to masturbate by crossing their legs and in this way exert a steady and rhythmic pressure on the whole genital area. They can do this in buses or other public conveyances, or even in the classroom, either by swinging their legs to cause the pressure or, less noticeably, simply by rhythmically tightening and relaxing their thigh muscles. This can also be done by lying face down, with buttocks moving rhythmically against each other, and with legs either crossed or uncrossed. Whether she also uses something beneath her, a pillow or part of the bedclothes, doesn't matter, since it's not the stimulation of something against the sex organ that brings her to orgasm, but rather the muscular tension in the body, resembling the tensions developed in the motions of intercourse.

Other ways of building up this muscular tension include climbing up a pole or a rope or even chinning on parallel bars. About 50 percent of women also discover that their breasts are erotically sensitive, and about one girl in ten stimulates her breast with one hand while she rubs her clitoris with the other. Few girls, however, can achieve orgasm by breast stimulation alone.

About 20 percent of girls insert something in their

vaginas to masturbate, but not many do this regularly. The most common object inserted is one or more fingers. When that's done, a girl pulls her hand up against the top of the organ so that the clitoris and the labia minora are stimulated at the same time. A few girls get more satisfaction out of deep vaginal penetration than they do from stimulating the clitoris, but the number is small. Most boys believe that inserting something is the way girls masturbate, because they think in terms of the penis being inserted into the vagina, and find it difficult to realize that the girl's area of erotic stimulation is her clitoris, not the vagina.

There are a variety of other techniques, including the use of a vibrator to stimulate the clitoris and the area around it, using fruits or vegetables like bananas or cucumbers to penetrate the vagina, or inserting objects into the anus. The vibrator has been found to be a very effective way for girls to achieve orgasm, and many of them are using this method more and more. There is no danger of getting "hooked" on it, as some people mistakenly believe. About 2 percent of girls are able to have orgasm by means of conscious fantasy alone. Only one boy in a thousand is able to do this.

If there's no attempt to delay the speed of orgasm, the average girl has a climax in less than four minutes, although some can do it in only a few seconds. Since in intercourse the male usually has some trouble holding back his orgasm until the girl is ready, it is advisable for boys to learn to delay it. This can be practiced in masturbation. For the same reason, it's good for girls *not* to delay it when they masturbate, even though they may find that they can go on and on and have two or more orgasms in succession.

When boys begin to masturbate, about the time they enter puberty, they tend to continue the experience regularly until some other kind of sexual activity begins. Even after they start to pet and have intercourse, they continue to masturbate with regularity, but with decreasing frequency.

Girls, on the other hand, tend to be much less regular about their masturbation. They may do it a great deal for a period of time, perhaps as often as twenty times a week or once a day for two months—and then they'll suddenly stop for a longer period of time. Stopping may be the result of guilt feelings, but more often it's simply a lack of interest. For quite a few girls, there seems to be an absence of sexual desire, a lack of pressure being built up because of limited sexual activity until it must explode in orgasm, as is the case with boys. Girls find it hard to understand that boys have this pressure, which is frequently with them, just as it sometimes seems incomprehensible to boys that girls can take sex or leave it alone so easily.

Another difference between the sexes lies in what girls think about while they masturbate. About a third of them don't appear to think about anything except the sensation itself. Girls who do fantasize usually think only of the experiences they've already had. For example, a girl who has only kissed with a boy and has gone no further will usually fantasize kissing a boy when she masturbates, while a boy who has only kissed will probably think of intercourse. Girls also tend to fantasize more general things, like living with a boy, or lying down with him, or being in some romantic setting. Boys are much more specific. They develop scenarios and almost always the genitals are involved in their fantasies.

Girls who do have specific sexual fantasies sometimes find them disturbing. They may think of intercourse with teachers, with their fathers or brothers, or they may imagine that they are prostitutes or are being raped. The only harm that can come from such fantasies is a feeling of guilt. Sex fantasies, like other daydreams, are part of normal life and should be regarded as such. Boys have these fantasies too. They imagine having sex with teachers or their sisters or even their mothers or fathers, and sometimes they imagine an orgy with several girls and boys, or perhaps just boys. They may think of having sex with a particular girl or boy, or a grown man or woman, or forcing someone else to have sex, or of being forced themselves. There is nothing wrong with fantasies about forcing, although it would be if they were carried out in reality. For example, I have never known a woman who consciously wanted to be raped, and women would certainly resist it in real life if resistance was possible, yet rape fantasies are quite common among girls and women.

Obviously, boys have a more elaborate fantasy life than girls, which is only natural because they're more preoccupied with sex. In either sex, the chances are low that any of these masturbation fantasies will ever come true, but they add to the excitement. When a girl or boy stops fantasizing and comes back to the real world, real things are dealt with in a realistic way and no harm is done.

Both girls and boys sometimes masturbate because of a conflict in their lives that is not sexual. Boredom, frustration, and loneliness are motivations too. Sometimes they do it because they have a poor opinion of themselves, don't know how to get along with the other sex, or find themselves in constant conflict with parents. If they're under great pressure at school, boys particularly tend to masturbate more. Masturbation does relieve the tension, whatever it is, temporarily, but if it seems that the primary motive for masturbation is any of these nonsexual reasons, youngsters ought to get some counseling help and try to solve their problems.

The only other source of sexual feeling I haven't mentioned is the activity that results from sexual dreams. This is far more prevalent among boys than girls. Few teenage girls have orgasms when they're asleep, although it's fairly common in older women, nearly half of whom do. For teenagers, however, the percentage is small. The sexual dreams girls have are about the same as the fantasies they have when they masturbate, and there are the same differences in the content of the girls' and boys' dreams as occur in fantasy.

In our complicated society, both girls and boys learn

early that there are many different attitudes about masturbation, as I indicated at the beginning of the chapter. They hear from their parents, either directly or by unspoken attitudes, that it's wrong or harmful to health, or both, if the parents happen to be traditional people. If the girl (or boy) is brought up in a strong religious faith, she will hear that masturbation distracts people from the true purpose of sexuality, marriage and reproduction, and that therefore it's wrong. Even those who don't take either of these attitudes may shrink from encouraging masturbation as something positive and good.

If they don't discover it by themselves, young girls and boys need to know that masturbation is not only harmless but positively good and healthy, and ought to be encouraged because it helps young people to grow up sexually in a natural way. More and more people are coming to understand and accept this.

It almost goes without saying, however, that we all learn as we grow up what's acceptable public behavior and what's acceptable only in private, and we learn quickly that masturbation is private. But we should also understand that because something is private doesn't mean it's bad or inferior or "dirty." Masturbating in private is a completely acceptable way of releasing sexual tension and an important part of growing up. It's not a substitute for anything else but an end in itself. Fear, anxiety, and guilt are the only harmful things about it. Once these are conquered, masturbation is a happy and useful experience.

CHAPTER 10
Lesbianism

Homosexual behavior is sexual behavior between people of the same sex. To understand it better, you should remember that for behavior to be sexual it must involve more than just physical contact and must result in some change in the body—deeper breathing, a warm skin, a rapid pulse, or some other symptom that can be identified as sexual. By this measurement, two girls walking arm in arm, or with their arms around each other, or kissing, are not necessarily involved in homosexual behavior, although they could be if they have sexual feelings for each other when they're doing it.

To define homosexual behavior more exactly, a woman who has sexual relations with another woman or who is aroused sexually by another woman is called a "lesbian." The word comes from the Greek island of Lesbos, where in ancient times the poet Sappho lived and wrote of the joys of lesbian love in glowing verse that has become part of the classical literature.

One thing that confuses a great many people is thinking of homosexuality as something separate and distinct from heterosexuality, which means sexual relations or attraction between members of opposite sexes. Because a girl is sexually aroused by or has relations with another girl doesn't mean she can't have relations with boys, just as a girl who likes ice cream may also like pie. A girl may be exclusively heterosexual, meaning she has never had any sexual contact with another girl or been aroused by one. Or she can be exclusively homosexual. There are probably 2 to 3 percent of girls who fall in the latter category. About a quarter fall between the two extremes; these girls have some combination of heterosexual and homosexual behavior in their lives. These are known as bisexuals.

A common occurrence in growing up is for a girl to become very fond of another girl and have warm, affectionate feelings toward her. We call it a "crush," an old-fashioned word for which there doesn't seem to be any modern substitute. Sometimes it's hard to draw the line between a crush and a sexual feeling. For example, I'm thinking of fourteen-year-old Jane, who is constantly in the company of her girl friend Betty. They spend hours together, talking about their experiences, their plans for the future, other girls, school, and the thousand things all girls find to talk about. They often put their arms around each other, and when they're separated during the summer vacation, they think about each other and write letters. They always feel especially good in each other's company. This is a typical picture of a schoolgirl crush, of the kind millions of girls have known. It's something almost all girls have experienced in one degree or another.

Up to this point, there's nothing homosexual in their behavior. But suppose that one night, while Jane is sleeping over with Betty at her house, they embrace each other in their customary warm, affectionate way and something happens that hasn't happened before. Sexual feelings are aroused. They begin to stroke each other's bodies, especially the breasts and sex organs, and experience sexual excitement from the contact. They may or may not have an orgasm as a result. It's at this point that the crush turns into a homosexual response.

Many girls have had such experiences, although they weren't lesbians. Their response to each other was no more than a sexual extension of their past relationship. Perhaps it only happened once or was repeated infrequently. On the other hand, girls with strong feelings for other girls, sexually and emotionally, may tend to become so absorbed in their sexual relationship with each other that they exclude physical and social contact with boys, and it may be that this will be their life preference. However, not all girls who turn out to be lesbians ignore boys. Many have warm and enduring friendships with the opposite sex throughout their lives.

As you can see, it isn't just sexual behavior with a member of the same sex that indicates a girl is a lesbian. What appears to be the determining factor is the amount and intensity of relating sexually and in other ways to members of the same sex.

It seems to me the important thing is that girls approach whatever sexual preference seems right for them in a positive way, not for negative reasons. If a girl relates to other girls because she's afraid of boys or because she wants to avoid dating so she won't have to face the problems it brings, the development of her homosexual life will be taking place for negative reasons. Or if she relates to boys because she's afraid of what others will say about her as a lesbian, the development of her heterosexual life will be taking place for negative reasons. I feel that all relationships, whether sexual or nonsexual, can only be sound if they are based on positive reasons.

One of the reasons for this book is to give young women information on human sexuality so they can make informed choices on many levels. Any life choice we make is extremely important. Girls who feel a strong pull to lesbianism, heterosexuality, or bisexuality need to know all the pros and cons of each so they can feel that their choice is made freely, knowingly, and positively—because it is the way of life they prefer.

Few people are able to accept the fact that everyone is *potentially* capable of doing every act imaginable, including having homosexual relations, given the proper circumstances, conditioning, and background. Everyone has homosexual tendencies in one degree or another, but it doesn't mean we will ever actually do anything about it or even be aware of it.

It's a common experience to be stirred by a sexual feeling toward someone of the same sex, through a fantasy, a dream, or in some other way. This idea horrifies most people. If they have such a conscious thought, they feel intensely guilty about their "perverted" feelings. Yet most people will never take part in a homosexual act, and their momentary thoughts or feelings will never interfere with their heterosexual lives. Once more, it's only guilt and fear that will plague them, if they permit it.

Nevertheless, girls are curious about lesbianism when they hear of it. They're at once repelled and fascinated. Often they ask, "But what do they *do*?" It may surprise them to know that they do what girls and boys do together, except that they don't have intercourse with a penis involved. Sometimes the sexual contact is no more than kissing, or tongue-kissing, but it may also include, and usually does, stroking the body and breasts, mutual masturbation, mouths on each other's sex organs, or lying together with sex organs against each other, going through the movements of intercourse.

Only about one girl in ten ever has specific homosexual contacts. Nearly twice that number are aroused psychologically in a specific sexual way by other girls. For the girls who have actual contact, the experience on the average is about once in five weeks. Usually the experiences occur in clusters, rather than spread out evenly, much like masturbation.

For various complicated reasons, there is more toleration for female homosexuals in our country than for males, although a homosexual act between two females is as illegal in some states as male homosexual behavior. Women are rarely arrested for homosexual behavior, much less convicted, except in the armed forces. In some other parts of the world, the reverse is true.

The reasons are various. Primarily it's because of our social inheritance from our Judeo-Christian ancestors, who regarded women as little more than property, and so female sexual behavior that did not affect males was of little concern to the lawmakers. Masturbation and homosexuality were virtually ignored among women. Again, homosexuality was early identified with anal intercourse, the preferred method among male homosexuals, so female homosexuality was not considered wrong. In our own time, people were not so much aware of lesbian behavior until the Gay Rights movement, involving both sexes, made them understand that the female homosexuals were emerging along with the males from the secret world they had inhabited before and were demanding to be treated equally with heterosexual people.

The general attitude of girls toward homosexual behavior among members of their own sex is more tolerant than corresponding attitudes among boys. However, girls are quick to condemn or reject other girls who don't do things the way they do or as the group does. The girl who wears a different kind of clothing or acts in a different way is often ostracized and rejected by the others. Everyone must conform to the fads and customs of the time or she's ridiculed. This is especially true when girls display any homosexual behavior. Ironically, it's their rejection by the rest of the group that often impels them to develop patterns of exclusive homosexuality, since they are then denied the possibility of heterosexuality.

One of the reasons we reject other people is fear of them or of what they might do; another is ignorance of their behavior. One of the things I hope this book will accomplish is to provide more information about homosexuality so that some of the fear and ignorance leading to the rejection of other people will be diminished a little. I believe people should be accepted or rejected on the basis of themselves as individuals, rather than whether they like ice cream or pie.

There are a few lesbians who develop mannish mannerisms, both in the way they dress and in their actions, but only about 5 percent of girls with active homosexual lives develop these characteristics. There are some girls whom we call "tomboys," but they usually have no homosexual inclinations at all. In a great majority of cases, it's impossible for a girl to tell whether or not her friends or acquaintances are engaged in homosexual behavior. About 15 percent of homosexual boys are obvious, which means that a girl will not be able, in most cases, to tell among the boys she knows which ones are involved in homosexual behavior.

Another common misconception is that in a lesbian

relationship one partner exclusively plays the male role and is called a "butch," while the other exclusively plays the "femme." Although this does occur, in the great majority of cases lesbians love each other without playing any "role" at all.

There are occasions when a girl is dating a boy and suspects he's having homosexual activity. Sometimes girls are so repulsed by the idea that they reject the boy, and this, of course, pushes him even further in the direction of homosexuality. My feeling is that if a girl accepts the boy as he is, without making an issue of his homosexuality or becoming a rival, there may still be a good possibility that she will be able to work out a satisfactory relationship with him and that his homosexuality will fall into proper perspective in his life. If I may go back to my familiar analogy—just as you don't learn to like ice cream by giving up pie, so you don't learn to like heterosexuality by giving up homosexuality. This applies to girls as well as to boys.

As I've noted, there are girls who like to dress in a mannish way, like boys; also there are a few other girls who dress like males and want to *become* males and think they *are* males. In a few cases, they even have operations to remove their breasts and have penises sewn to their bodies so that they can perform as males. These are called "transsexuals." Most girls will probably never meet such a person. Much more common are males who want to become females; there are several thousand cases of men who have been operated on successfully to accomplish this transformation.

The noted British writer James Morris wrote a book called *Conundrum* about the experience by which he was transformed to Jan Morris.

Girls are sometimes faced with having a crush on an older woman, especially a teacher. It can be very flattering to have an older woman take a personal interest in a girl, and most girls have had this experience in one degree or another. These relationships are often happy and helpful ones to a girl growing up, and they rarely lead to any sexual activity, as some adults fear.

When sex does become the aim of the older woman's advances, whether or not she's a teacher, the situation is quite different from when an older man makes a sexual approach. An older woman's approach will be much more gradual and gentle.

It's usually easier for a girl to say no to an older woman than to put off the older man. If she's confronted with this problem, the girl should ask herself the same question she did about the man: why does this older person want to be involved with a young girl?

In conclusion, I want to emphasize that homosexual relationships can be as pleasurable, as deep, and as worthwhile as heterosexual relationships, even though our society still has strong feelings against homosexual people. Because there are so many variables to consider, it seems to me that girls should be very sure of themselves and how they really feel about their sexual preference before they make such an important decision about the way their lives will be lived.

CHAPTER 11
Questions and Answers

If there are questions girls want to ask about sex that haven't been answered in the preceding pages, I hope they'll be answered here. These are questions that have actually been asked by several different groups of young girls. Readers may not find their own special questions, because obviously it would be impossible to set down the hundreds that might be asked. I urge readers who still have questions to seek the answers from a competent authority. To know is better than to wonder and imagine.

1. *Do boys have a different interest in sex from girls and a different ability to perform sexually?*

I've answered the first part of this question to some extent, but I can add that there are boys who, like girls, are "late bloomers" in the sense that they're not interested in sex until their late teens, then have an active sex life. I had one patient, twenty-four years old, who had never had an erection in his life because he was low in male hormones. But then there are boys who seem to be interested in sex almost from the time they are born. They learn quickly to masturbate to orgasm and may do so several times a day. Sometimes they continue an active sexual life until they are old men. Most boys fall between these extremes. With both boys and girls, if an individual is a highly sexed person, there isn't much that can be done to decrease his or her activity, even if that were desired, and conversely, if you're at the low end of the scale, not much can be done to increase sexual activity to any appreciable extent. People should accept their sexuality, whatever it is, no matter where they fall on the scale.

2. *How long can sperm live?*

They can live in the vagina from one to two days. Some have been kept alive, under special conditions, for eight days or more. When sperm are not in a warm, moist, alkaline place, they die quickly.

3. *What is circumcision?*

Girls are often curious about this, especially if they've had a chance to see the different appearance of a penis when this operation has been performed. There is a loose piece of skin extending to the end or beyond the end of the penis. This is called the "foreskin." Doctors often cut it off a few days after a baby is born. The procedure is common in hospitals today, and it's called "circumcision." Not many males of this generation are uncircumcised. Circumcision is done in the belief that it's easier to keep the head of the penis and the part just beyond it cleaner, although actually there is nothing unclean about an uncircumcised man's penis.

The Jewish religion requires that the male be circumcised and the operation itself is a religious ritual.

There are other reasons, too, for circumcision. Sometimes the foreskin sticks to the head of the penis (this is called "adhesion") and circumcision is required to get it unstuck. In other cases, the foreskin has such a small opening that the head of the penis cannot be pushed through. This condition is called "phimosis." Sometimes it's possible to stretch the foreskin without circumcision. Boys also have to contend with a white cheeselike substance forming behind the head of the penis, called "smegma." It may have to be washed away sometimes because it has an unpleasant odor.

4. *What is "stone ache" or "lover's nuts"?*

In the chapter on orgasm I explained that girls may get an ache in the groin because they have petted heavily or masturbated but not to the point of orgasm, when sexual tension is relieved. This also happens to boys. They too get aches in the groin when they have been petting for a long time with erection but without orgasm. Boys believe these aches to be in their testicles and call this condition by the slang terms above. Its cause in both sexes is congestion, which leads to muscle contraction. It's the aching of these contracted muscles that is felt as pain.

5. *What is impotence?*

It's something girls don't have to worry about as far as their own anatomy is concerned, but it's a serious problem where their sexual partners are involved. The most common kind of impotence is erectile impotence, in which the male cannot get an erection. It may happen to a young boy when he's frightened or if he's fearful he may not be able to get one. Less common is ejaculatory impotence, which happens when a male can get an erection but is unable to ejaculate. Impotence is usually caused by anxiety and disappears when the causes of the anxiety are removed.

6. *What are other common words for the penis?*

Girls are likely to hear at least some of the long list of synonyms for penis. Most commonly they may hear it called a "cock," "dick," "peter," "pecker," "dong," or "wee-wee."

7. *What are other words for testicles?*

Again, this will clear up some mysterious references girls hear in conversation or read in books. The two most common synonyms are "balls" and "nuts," but there are many others. Girls are likely to be much more familiar with all these words today, since they appear so commonly in print.

8. *What are other names for masturbation?*

One or two are used in common by both sexes, like "playing with yourself," but most of the others are more commonly used by boys, words like "jacking off," "jerking off," and "beating your meat." Today both sexes also use that ambiguous phrase, "getting it off," which has several other meanings.

9. *What are other words for sexual intercourse?*

Among the words acceptable in society are the two used by doctors and those who write seriously about sex—"coitus" and "copulation." The other synonyms —and there are literally hundreds of them, since these are among the most common words in the English language—have not been accepted until recently, but now many of them appear in movies, the theater, in some newspapers and magazines, and all of them can be found in popular novels. A few of the more common words are "fuck," "screw," "lay," "sleep with," "jellyroll," "poontang," and "jazz"—the latter three being part of black slang.

10. *What is the vagina?*

To repeat a little, the vagina is a tubelike structure, about three and a half inches in depth, extremely expandable. The penis enters it during intercourse. The whole structure of the female sex organ, including the vulva and the vagina, has many other names in common usage, just as the penis does. Among the most common are "cunt" and "pussy."

11. *What is the clitoris?*

Again to repeat, in case anyone missed it earlier, the clitoris is a small, pealike structure at the top of the inner lips of the vulva enfolded by the outer lips. It's the female equivalent of the male penis and is the focal point of stimulation in masturbation and petting. A slang term for clitoris is "man in the boat."

12. *Are there times when a girl either doesn't want to or can't have intercourse?*

The times when a girl *wants* intercourse vary greatly from girl to girl, but on the average, girls are more aroused for the day or two just before they menstruate, and a little less so again for the day or two following menstruation. A third likely time is during the menstrual period. This, however, is not true for every girl. There are those who don't vary much in their sexual feeling. While there's no harm in having intercourse when a girl is menstruating, many don't want to have it then because they have cramps, because they think it's too messy, or because of social taboos. This is especially true of those who follow the Jewish religion, which considers it unclean and wrong. When they feel like having sex, girls are usually reacting more to the mood or the occasion. Quite naturally, if they've just had a quarrel with a boy or they're feeling sulky or pouty about something, or if the time and place just don't seem right to them, they're not likely to want even to pet, much less to have intercourse. Occasionally, too, there are medical reasons why a girl should not have intercourse, particularly when she has an infection in her vagina or urethra.

13. *Do particular foods or drugs pep up the sex drive?*

The answer is no. If a girl wants to stimulate her sex drive (and not many would think of doing anything about it), she should get plenty of sleep, eat good, nourishing food, and in general keep in good health. Among the old wives' tales about this subject is the superstition that foods like raw oysters, eggs, or malted milk stimulate sexual interest. There's no truth in this idea. A girl should never permit a boy, or permit herself, to use the powdered drug known as "Spanish fly," or cantharides. It's commonly believed that the application of this drug will make the female extremely excited sexually, but what it actually does is to irritate the lining of the urethra, and if it's taken in sufficient quantity, it's highly poisonous. It has no effect on sexuality. For centuries people have looked for medicines or drugs to help stimulate them or their partners sexually. Nothing has ever been found that will do it, except the injection of male hormones, and unfortunately this procedure may have dangerous side effects.

14. *What is a "cherry"?*

This is the slang term for the hymen. The fact that it's erroneously believed that hymens are never broken until penetrated by the male penis leads to such other slang phrases as "picking a cherry," or "getting a cherry." By this is meant that a boy has had intercourse with a virgin, that is, a girl who has never had intercourse before and so, it is presumed incorrectly, must have an intact hymen.

15. *What is a whore?*

This very old name is applied to a girl or woman who has intercourse for money. The technical name is "prostitute." But again, there are synonyms: "hustlers," "streetwalkers," and "call girls," among others. Sometimes the word "whore," like "slut," is used to mean a "bad woman."

16. *What is a pimp?*

A pimp is a man who manages a prostitute and takes a part or all of her earnings. He is her business manager in a sense, occasionally getting customers for her, but usually not. In common usage, however, "to pimp" means getting something illegally for someone else, and is also sometimes used as a general term of contempt for a man who is weak, shifty, or worthless.

17. *What is a male prostitute?*

A man who has sexual relations with another man for money. In male prostitution, the customer pays for the privilege of having the prostitute ejaculate. There are also a few male prostitutes who are paid by women.

18. *What is a hermaphrodite?*

A true hermaphrodite is one who has the gonads of both sexes (that is, testicles and ovaries). Few of these individuals exist, but there are pseudohermaphrodites who are anatomically somewhere between the two sexes: a boy with a tiny penis, like a clitoris, perhaps; or a girl with a large clitoris, almost large enough to be a penis. Corrective surgery can often make such a person more like a male or a female. Other pseudohermaphrodites may be a man who has large breasts like a woman's, a woman with no breasts at all, or a woman with hair on her face, like a man—the "bearded woman" of the circus and the carnival sideshow. These people are not really hermaphrodites. The trouble usually lies in a hormone imbalance. People often use corruptions of the word, like "amorphadite" or "morphadite" because they don't know the correct word, "hermaphrodite."

19. *What is castration?*

Once more, something girls need have no fear of, because it means cutting off the gonads of males. Since these are the main source of male hormones, an adolescent boy who has been castrated will have no growth of hair on his face, and the rest of his body hair will become fine and silky, while his voice remains high. He can't ejaculate and often can't get an erection. The word for such a person is "eunuch" (pronounced *yew'-nuk*). The older a man is, the less effect there will be if he's castrated. The equivalent operation in females would be removal of the ovaries, making them unable to have children.

20. *What are common names for gonorrhea?*

Most often used are "the clap" and "the drips."

21. *What are common names for syphilis?*

Most often used are "the syph," "blue balls," and "bad blood," although there are several others.

22. *What is abnormal sex?*

I can't really answer this question, even though the phrase is used so much, because the word "abnormal" is so ambiguous. Let me show you what I mean. The word can mean something that's unusual or rare, so by that definition it would be abnormal to have intercourse by hanging from the chandelier because, I think it's safe to say, very few people have intercourse in this position. By that definition, however, masturbation would have to be considered normal because most boys and girls masturbate. Homosexuality, too, would be almost normal because so many are involved in it.

Another way of defining "abnormal" is to say that it's anything which is unnatural. Since human sexual behavior is like that of other animals, it's natural. All mammals, of which humans are a species, engage in practically every kind of sex, including petting, masturbation, and homosexuality, so by this definition there is essentially nothing humans do sexually that is abnormal.

A third way to look at "abnormal" is through the eyes of society. We can look to both our laws and our churches for guidance here, although they are not always in complete agreement, and some churches today are much more liberal than they used to be. For example, it isn't against the law to masturbate, except in public, but some religions think it's wrong. On the other hand, it's against the law in about half the states to put your mouth on the sex organ of another person. Many religious leaders don't believe this is wrong, and many husbands and wives, as well as a great many other people, do it.

Still another way to look at "abnormal" is to consider what sexual acts harm other people. Things like forcing other people to engage in sexual behavior against their will, or lying, cheating, or seducing them into doing what they don't want to do would be considered abnormal.

It's easy to see, then, what a complicated business it is trying to decide what is abnormal sex, and that's why I suggest that the question can't be answered.

23. *What is a wet dream?*

This is something that most often happens to boys, but it can happen to girls as well, as I've remarked in the chapter on masturbation. For the boy, he wakes up some night or in the morning to discover that he's had an ejaculation while he was asleep. This may puzzle or frighten some boys who have heard that loss of semen in sleep is somehow damaging, which of course is not true. The "wet dream" is simply the result of sexual excitement caused by dreaming, which eventually reaches the usual climax, with the emission of semen (for boys). It isn't, as some think, an automatic substitute for intercourse or even a means of relieving sexual tension. In fact, it may often follow a sexual experience.

24. *What is adultery, and what is fornication?*

Adultery is sexual experience when one or both persons are married but not to each other. Fornication is intercourse when neither partner is married. These are legal terms. In all the states, adultery is against the law, and in about half of them fornication is illegal.

25. *What would happen if a human being had intercourse with an animal?*

In spite of all the legends and fairy tales about it, no pregnancy will occur. In fact, about one out of five boys who live on farms or visit one during summer vacation have intercourse, or attempt it, with animals. Only one or two of a hundred boys who live in cities ever practice such behavior. Any of the farm animals may become a sexual object—ponies, calves, sheep, pigs, even chickens or ducks. Dogs are also used, but cats rarely. Intercourse with animals is usually infrequent among the boys who practice it, but some build up a strong emotional attachment to a particular animal and have intercourse with it on a regular basis. This behavior is against the law in nearly every state, and very severe penalties are provided for violation, not to mention the social ridicule which accompanies its discovery. Technically, intercourse with animals is called "bestiality."

While there are cases of girls having sexual activity, or even intercourse, with animals, especially dogs, it's much rarer than among boys. However, the incidence is as high among urban females as males, while the ratio is four times as high among rural males as opposed to females.

26. *Can human beings and animals mate and have young?*

They can mate, as indicated above, but they can't become pregnant. Animals of different species, however, do sometimes mate and, if they are similar enough, can have offspring—for example, tigers and lions, buffalo and domestic cattle. But human beings aren't close enough to any other animal to have offspring.

27. *What is "69"?*

This is the slang name for the position in sexual play where both male and female have mouth-genital contact at the same time.

28. *What is sadomasochism?*

This is a contraction of two words, "sadism," meaning to get sexual pleasure from giving pain to someone, and "masochism," meaning to get sexual pleasure from pain inflicted by someone else—in both cases, with the consent of each party. The words are combined because most people who get sexual pleasure from hurting others also get it from being hurt. People often use these words in a nonsexual way, applying "sadist" to people who seem to enjoy hurting other people and "masochist" to those who appear to get satisfaction out of being humiliated. This, however, is really an incorrect usage.

There is a little sadomasochism in all of us. For example, people who are aroused sexually often enjoy nibbling, biting, or scratching. A few people develop much stronger behavior in this direction. They enjoy being beaten, whipped, tied down, or similar treatment. Boys and girls sometimes think of such activity when they masturbate or at other times. But there is no cause to worry unless these things are put into practice.

29. *What is incest?*

Legally, incest is having sexual intercourse with a relative of the opposite sex. This relative could be mother, father, brother, sister, grandparent or grandchild, and in some states, uncles or aunts or first cousins. It usually includes stepparents, stepchildren, stepbrothers, and stepsisters, even though they are not blood relatives. It includes adopted children.

In its broader sense, however, incest doesn't necessarily mean sexual intercourse, but includes any kind of sexual relations, even homosexual, between relatives. Sex play with sisters and cousins, however, is not at all unusual in preadolescence.

The incest taboo is the oldest of them all, going back to earliest times, and it's the strongest. Guilt alone makes a strong inhibition, and, of course, all religions absolutely forbid it. There are also medical reasons for the taboo, or at least that was believed until recently. It was said that the children of an incestuous union would be likely to inherit the outstanding bad characteristics of both parents, but genetically, so it was said, continuing incestuous relationships in a group would tend to "breed out"—that is, the bad traits would eventually overcome the good ones in successive generations. Recent research, however, has cast considerable doubt on these long-held beliefs, and some scientists now think there is no basis for them.

30. *Should children be allowed to run around the house without any clothes on?*

It's one of the paradoxes of human life that we are told constantly and in many ways how beautiful the human body is, yet we're ashamed to show it in front of other people except within certain limits, of which the bikini is the extreme. This need to cover the body is as old as Adam, in one sense. Originally people covered themselves as protection from the weather, but in time it became a matter of religion, and in our own society it's a heritage from the strict religious feelings of the early colonists, whose Puritanism, as we call it now, set the tone of American life in its moral aspects. Consequently, people can't be as free as some might like to be, short of joining a nudist colony, because they will feel the weight of society's displeasure. It's possible to be more relaxed about nudity in the privacy of the home—if, in that home, the standards are different from those in society at large. Parents will set these standards for the most part. To a large extent, they determine how much nudity is permitted, and where and when. No matter what is decreed, the human body remains beautiful and one need feel no shame in viewing it.

31. *What is a douche (pronounced* doosh)?

In Chapter 8, I mentioned the douche as a means of washing out semen from the vagina in order not to become pregnant. Douching for this purpose is highly ineffective. Most doctors believe too frequent douching can be harmful because it washes out natural lubricating liquids from the vagina. Unless there's some infection, most physicians advise against it. However, some girls do it for reasons of cleanliness. Washing with soap and water outside the sex organ to cleanse the secretions that form particularly around the clitoris and inner lips is sufficient.

32. *What is a miscarriage?*

A miscarriage (sometimes called a "spontaneous abortion") is the loss of the fetus before it's able to live outside the mother.

Some causes relate to the physical condition of the mother, like certain types of fibroid tumors, tears in the womb mouth from childbirth, or a misshapen uterus. Others result from general illnesses, like abnormal gland function, chronic high blood pressure, uncontrolled diabetes, untreated syphilis, severe undernourishment, and high fevers. Careful medical supervision can forestall miscarriage in diabetics and women with high blood pressure.

These physical causes are involved in the minority of miscarriages. Most miscarriages result from what is called by doctors "defective germ plasm." Almost three out of four human miscarriages are the result of defective eggs. A fetus that develops improperly usually dies and is expelled from the body as foreign material by muscular contractions of the uterus. A defective-germ-plasm conception usually stops developing after six or seven weeks, but is carried in the uterus for three or four weeks longer. Consequently, a miscarriage occurs usually around the tenth or eleventh week of pregnancy.

Contrary to popular opinion, few miscarriages are caused by a blow or jolt or an emotional upheaval. Most doctors agree, as one specialist puts it, that "you cannot shake a good human egg loose, any more than a fresh wind will cause healthy unripe apples to fall from the tree."

Miscarriage usually offers virtually no risk to a woman, although she may bleed enough to require a transfusion, and she should recover in a few days.

33. *What is sodomy?*

The word comes from the biblical town of Sodom, the sinful city, in which people were supposed to be involved in "unnatural sexual practices." We have no idea what these practices really were. Sodomy has sometimes meant any homosexual practice, or putting the mouth on the sex organ of another person, whether in homosexual or heterosexual contact, or any anal intercourse whether homosexual or heterosexual, or any contact between humans and other animals.

34. *What does the expression "female trouble" mean?*

It refers to any sort of physical complaint women have in connection with their sex organs. This would include trouble with menstruation, the vagina, the ovaries, or the uterus.

35. *What does "caesarean section" mean?*

It's the birth of a baby through the abdominal wall. The uterus is cut open and the baby is taken directly out of it without passing through the vagina. This is done if the baby is too large or is in the wrong position, or if the mother has some physical condition that would make regular birth too difficult. In modern medical practice, it isn't a dangerous operation and many women have perfectly healthy babies delivered by this method.

36. *Does a man ever urinate in a woman during intercourse?*

It's very difficult, though not impossible, for a man to urinate with an erect penis, and it's hard to have intercourse without an erection. Consequently, it happens only rarely.

37. *What does a man do when he rapes a woman?*

"To rape" means "to have intercourse by force." Theoretically, it's impossible to rape a woman, but there are all kinds of possible force. For example, if a man were to pin a woman down with his body and struggle with her for a long time so she would give in, then had intercourse with her, that would be considered rape. Again, the use of a weapon to threaten a woman into submitting would be rape. According to law, a girl who is under a certain age (in some states it's sixteen, in others as high as twenty-one) is technically unable to give consent. Thus, any intercourse, even if a girl is willing, is called "statutory rape," or "rape with consent," if she is under the prescribed age.

38. *What is a fetus?*

Any unborn baby. Up to seven weeks, this is also known as an "embryo."

39. *How does artificial insemination work?*

Sometimes the husband can't make his wife pregnant, because he hasn't manufactured enough sperm, or because the sperm dies before reaching the egg, or for several other reasons, some physical and some psychological. In these cases, it's sometimes possible to inject his semen into his wife artificially and she becomes pregnant. In other cases, it's necessary to use the semen of another man. This can be placed in the vagina by the doctor in his or her office. The woman never sees the donor. Consequently, there are women who have babies without having their husbands impregnate them. It's estimated that about 10,000 children are born this way in the United States every year.

40. *What is the difference in pubic hair between men and women?*

A woman's is finer and silkier, like the hair on her head. A woman's pubic hair is also distributed more in the shape of a triangle, wider at the top. Some boys think they can tell if the color of a girl's hair is natural if it's the same color as her pubic hair. Actually, the real comparison is with the eyebrows. A blond girl's pubic hair will tend to be darker than her head hair, a brunette's will be lighter. As people get older, pubic hair tends to become gray, although at a much slower rate than head hair.

In boys, the hair grows around the penis, especially directly above it; and in some boys, as they grow older, a line of hair grows up to the navel. This is called the "linea alba." A few girls also have this line. There is also some pubic hair that grows from a boy's scrotum, and even in back of it, to and around the anus.

A girl's pubic hair doesn't interfere with intercourse because there is none on the inner lip of the vulva or even on the inside of the outer lips.

41. *How does a hospital determine if a girl has been raped?*

In reality, it can't tell. It can determine if she's had intercourse recently, if there's still some semen in the vagina. Bruises or scratches, freshly inflicted, may indicate the use of force. If a girl's hymen has been broken by the act, it may still be bleeding, or there will be traces of it, and this is another piece of evidence. But as we've seen in Question 37, it would be difficult to determine, in a physical sense, whether rape has occurred or not.

42. *Suppose a girl has intercourse and menstruates some time afterward. Is she pregnant?*

A few girls menstruate a time or two after they become pregnant, but in the great majority of cases, it stops when pregnancy begins.

43. *What is menopause?*

Menopause, or "change of life," or "the change," should be understood by girls (and by boys too) because their mothers will be experiencing it. Between forty-five and fifty-five, usually, women stop producing an egg cell every month. This is not a serious loss at that age, especially since menstruation will also cease. However, the female hormone (estrogen) may also somewhat diminish and this may produce uncomfortable feelings. Physicians have learned how to treat this normal stage of a woman's life with additional hormones. In any case, contrary to popular belief, her sexual life will not change but will go on exactly as it was before menopause.

Afterword

I want to add a word here about sex in relation to a girl's life, since it doesn't exist as something separate and apart from day-to-day living. It's true that sex is very important, but it's unrealistic to overemphasize it. The amount of time a girl spends thinking about sex, even in adolescence, when it all seems new and exciting, usually takes up only a small part of her thoughts. Her actual sexual activity is likely to be even less, unlike an adolescent boy's—and even for him, sexual thoughts and activity are going to take up only a relatively small part of a total day.

If a girl masturbates, she probably won't be doing it as often as a boy, and when she dates, the sexual part of an evening, if any, may be only a small part of it. Girls, as I've said, generally tend to take a much more romantic view of sex in these early years than boys do; they are already process-oriented, just as the boys are goal-oriented, where sex is concerned.

For anyone, sex is clearly an important part of life but it's a rather small part of the whole. If girls or boys spend a good part of their waking hours thinking about sex or doing something sexual, it's often because they're upset about it—feeling guilty, or anxious, or unsure. I hope this book will relieve girls of some of those guilt feelings, anxieties, and uncertainties, and that may decrease the amount of time they spend thinking about sex, or being actively engaged in it.

I'm not suggesting that it's better not to become involved with sex. On the contrary, I believe that it's both worthwhile and pleasurable, as I'm sure this book demonstrates. But if a girl feels guilty or anxious about it, something valuable is lost—something that can make her feel one inch small or ten feet high.

There's one important thing to remember: It isn't what you do sexually that matters, *as long as you're not hurting someone else;* it's how you *feel* about what you're doing. If you learn nothing else from these pages, that fact alone can make the difference between leading a whole life or only part of one.

Both girls and boys discover as they grow up that society tries to restrict what they're allowed to do sexually, but at the same time constantly stimulates their sexual interest through advertising, clothing, motion pictures, magazines, and television. They find themselves in a world that seems to be preoccupied by sex yet imposes strict prohibitions which remain a threat even though they're violated every day in the week.

You may be surprised to know that your grandparents knew something about that situation. In their day, everyone knew a familiar rhyme, all but forgotten now:

Mother, may I go out to swim?
Yes, my darling daughter;
Hang your clothes on a hickory limb,
But don't go near the water.

I hope this book will teach you how to swim without
drowning in a social sea that may not be nearly as angry
and restrictive as it was in your grandmother's or even
your mother's day, but may be twice as confusing.

Index

169

About the Author

WARDELL B. POMEROY received the A.B. and M.A. in psychology from Indiana University, and the Ph.D. from Columbia University. As research associate at the Institute for Sex Research, he was co-author with the late Alfred Kinsey of *Sexual Behavior in the Human Male* and *Sexual Behavior in the Human Female*. He is academic dean at the Institute for Advanced Study of Human Sexuality in San Francisco, California, where he lives with his family.